Preface and acknowledgements

This book was largely written in the summer of 1985. Its starting point was some research carried out for the British Association of Nature Conservationists and the World Wildlife Fund in 1983 on the way in which the Wildlife and Countryside Act 1981 was being implemented. In the three years since then, the acronym-ridden terminology of the Act has repeatedly been headline news. The question of how to conserve sites rich in wildlife in the context of intensifying agricultural, forestry and urban or industrial land uses has been highlighted by events time and again. The subject is more critical now than at any time in the past decade.

This book offers an analysis of the state of site protection in British nature conservation, but no simple prescription to solve the very real problems of conflict between conservation and other land uses. This is not an omission, simply a belief that there is no magic wand to be waved which will make the problems go away. However, that is not the end of the story. The problems, intractable though they are, *are* soluble, albeit not without some enlightened lateral thinking on several fronts. Hopefully, anyone reading this book will be clearer about what the problems are and where they come from. This must be the first step in the all-important search for solutions.

I would like to thank those who have made information available to me, and allowed me to take up their time with discussions and questions. I am particularly grateful to those in the Nature Conservancy Council, whose openness at a critical period (and on a sensitive subject) is both remarkable and creditable. I would also like to thank those who have been kind enough to read and comment on the manuscript, especially Richard Munton, Chris Rose, Derek Ratcliffe, Tim O'Riordan, John Sheail, Alan Vittery and Miles Jackson. Some of their suggestions I have acted on, others I have let lie, often because to do justice to them would really require another book. All errors and omissions which remain in the text are mine, but a number of the best ideas in the book are borrowed, I hope constructively. All opinions are obviously mine alone. I would like to thank Mike Young and Ian Gulley for drawing the figures, and my wife Franc for all her work on the proofs, and for generally keeping me sane.

The following individuals and organisations have kindly given permission for the reproduction of specific illustrations (figure numbers in parentheses):

William Dawson and M. Turner (1.2); the Nature Conservancy Council (1.3, 1.9, 1.10); the Institute of Terrestrial Ecology (1.4); Longman (1.5); the Botanical Society of the British Isles (1.6, 1.7); Elsevier Applied Science Publishers and G. P. Buckley (3.5); Figure 3.6 reproduced with the permission of the Controller, Her Majesty's Stationery Office, Crown copyright reserved.

Nature's PLACE

Conservation sites and countryside change

W. M. ADAMS

London
ALLEN & UNWIN
Boston   Sydney

Allen & Unwin (Publishers) Ltd,
40 Museum Street, London WC1A 1LU, UK

Allen & Unwin (Publishers) Ltd,
Park Lane, Hemel Hempstead, Herts HP2 4TE, UK

Allen & Unwin, Inc.,
8 Winchester Place, Winchester, Mass. 01890, USA

Allen & Unwin (Australia) Ltd,
8 Napier Street, North Sydney, NSW 2060, Australia

First published in 1986

British Library Cataloguing in Publication Data

Adams, W. M.
    Nature's place: conservation sites and countryside change.
1. Nature conservation – Great Britain
I. Title
333.76′16′0941   QH77.G7
ISBN 0-04-719009-4
ISBN 0-04-719010-8

Library of Congress Cataloging-in-Publication Data

Adams, W. M. (William Mark), 1955–
    Nature's Place
Bibliography: p.
Includes index.
1. Nature conservation – Great Britain. 2. Wildlife
conservation – Great Britain. 3. Nature conservation –
Law and legislation – Great Britain. 4. Wildlife
conservation – Law and legislation – Great Britain.
I. Title.
QH 77.G7A55 1986   333.95′16′.0941   86-8049
ISBN 0-04-7190094
ISBN 0-04-7190108 (pbk.)

Set in 10 on 11 point Sabon by Computape (Pickering) Limited,
Pickering, North Yorkshire
and printed in Great Britain by Billing and Son Ltd, London and
Worcester

List of tables

Acronyms and abbreviations

ADAS	Agricultural Development and Advisory Service
APAS	Alternative Package of Agricultural Subsidies
ARO	Assistant Regional Officer
CAP	Common Agricultural Policy
CC	Countryside Commission
CLA`	Country Landowners Association
CPO	Compulsory Purchase Order
CPRE	Council for the Protection of Rural England
CRC	Countryside Review Committee
CTT	Capital Transfer Tax
DOE	Department of the Environment
EEC	European Economic Community
ESA	Environmentally Sensitive Area
FC	Forestry Commission
FEOGA	European Agricultural Guidance and Guarantee Fund
FOE	Friends of the Earth
FWAG	Farming and Wildlife Advisory Group
ITE	Institute of Terrestrial Ecology
LFA	Less Favoured Area
MAFF	Ministry of Agriculture, Fisheries and Food
NC	Nature Conservancy
NCC	Nature Conservancy Council
NCO	Nature Conservation Order
NERC	Natural Environment Research Council
NFU	National Farmers Union
NGO	Non-governmental Organisation
NNR	National Nature Reserve
NRA	Nature Reserve Agreement
NRIC	Nature Reserves Investigations Committee
PDO	Potentially Damaging Operation
PSSSI	Proposed Site of Special Scientific Interest
RASE	Royal Agricultural Society of England
RSNC	Royal Society for Nature Conservation

Contents

Contents

Acronyms and abbreviations

RSPB	Royal Society for the Protection of Birds
RSPCA	Royal Society for the Prevention of Cruelty to Animals
SPNC	Society for the Promotion of Nature Conservation
SPNR	Society for the Promotion of Nature Reserves
SRDB	Site related data base
SSSI	Site of Special Scientific Interest
WCS	World Conservation Strategy

Introduction

There are no truly natural areas left in Britain. Everything except remote cliff ledges has been affected either directly or indirectly by man. None the less, there are still places where a great diversity of wild species survive, either largely independent of man, or under benign management. As the great ecologist and conservationist Arthur Tansley put it in 1939, 'Nature is always trying to restore some sort of equilibrium, and given sufficient time she succeeds in establishing new communities, into the organisation of which the human factor may enter to a greater or a lesser degree'.

These areas of semi-natural habitat were already limited and shrinking in the 1930s when Tansley wrote. He valued enormously those patches which remained, both as a scientist and as an individual, for their beauty and the simple pleasure they gave. Tansley was one of the people who worked to establish a government organisation in Britain responsible for nature conservation in the 1940s. He lived to be the first chairman of the Nature Conservancy (NC) from its establishment in 1949 until 1952.

In 1949, when the Nature Conservancy was created, the word 'conservation' meant very little to most people. Now, over three and a half decades later, it is widely understood, and many people call themselves 'conservationists'. Yet today many of the small areas of semi-natural habitat which had survived to Tansley's time have been destroyed. The countryside left to us in the 1980s is far less rich in wildlife than it was before the war, and animals and plants which were once common have become rare or have disappeared. This has happened in spite of the tremendous rise in interest in nature conservation which has taken place in Britain: indeed we have lost many of the very finest areas of wild and semi-natural habitat within just the past few decades. The erosion of what remains is still going on, and the pace of loss has, if anything, accelerated over the past five years.

Tony Patterson, in his pamphlet *Conservation and the Conservatives* which was published in 1984, chided the Conservative government for its piecemeal achievements in conservation, and said that the casualty list of lost wildlife sites read 'rather like *The Times* of July 1916'. Indeed, although the Wildlife and Countryside Act 1981 was intended (among many other things) to halt the loss of valuable sites, habitat loss remains an extremely serious problem. A Bill to amend the 1981 Act came before the House of Lords in June 1985. In the debate, Lord Buxton said 'since 1981 there has been more bitterness, more aggravation, more friction, and indeed a worsening of the type of relationships which are likely to prevent good conservation than there ever was before'. His is a pessimistic view, but without doubt the question of the loss of wildlife sites, and in particular the impact of the agricultural and forestry industries, has become politicised and publicised over the past five years in a way that has never happened before.

This book is about the debate over habitat loss. It examines the way it has developed, and the prospects for the future. The Chairman of the Nature Conservancy Council (NCC), in the Eleventh Report for the year 1984–5, takes a more hopeful line than for some years, but the NCC's own publication *Nature conservation in Great Britain* (published in 1984), gives a grim picture of the balance between success and failure in nature conservation since 1949. It suggests that the most serious failure of the conservation movement is the sheer scale of loss or damage to wildlife and wildlife habitats since the war. This book is essentially about that failure.

Chapter 1 puts the problem of habitat loss in perspective, and looks at the effects on wildlife habitats of changes in the countryside over time from the enclosures of the 19th century to the present day. Chapter 2 looks at the conservation organisations which developed from the same period, and their response to changes in wildlife populations and the countryside. It describes the way they increasingly chose to try to defend wildlife habitats by protecting particular selected areas against damage, by establishing nature reserves and, at a later date, Sites of Special Scientific Interest (SSSIs). This chapter moves from the 19th century to the 1940s, when debate about the countryside was wide-ranging and intense, eventually giving rise to fundamental legislation in the postwar period. Chapter 3 describes the developments in conservation which followed, from the end of the war to the point at the end of the 1970s when new legislation to try to stop habitat loss was at last seriously discussed. Over this period, habitat loss came to dominate thinking on conservation in Britain, and the debate led eventually to the introduction of the Wildlife and Countryside Bill to Parliament in 1980.

Chapter 4 describes the passage of that Bill through Parliament, and the implications and outcome of the stormy debate about the extent and significance of habitat loss, and the way to protect sites. The evolution of the Bill in Parliament is discussed, and the provisions of the Act which was eventually passed are described in detail. Chapter 5 then looks at the problem of making the provisions of the Act for the protection of SSSIs' work, and assesses their success. This outlines in detail the work of the Nature Conservancy Council (NCC) and the procedures which are used to protect SSSIs. In Chapter 6 the financial implications of the Act are discussed. The eventual cost is hard to predict, but will undoubtedly be great. The amount of money available for conservation in the countryside is compared with that supporting intensive agricultural and forestry activities, and it is argued that the imbalance goes a long way to explaining the problems which dog attempts to halt habitat loss. The final chapter (Ch. 7) looks forward to the future prospects of wildlife habitats, and outlines the kind of policies which will be necessary if the tragically poor record of conservation to date is to be improved.

This book concentrates on the conservation of nature and wildlife in the countryside, not the conservation of landscape or (a terrible weasel word) of 'amenity'. Of course, the natural beauty of wildlife habitats cannot be completely separated from their interest to naturalists or scientists, and few people seriously suggest that it can be. A landscape without wildlife, even if it is green and carefully organised, has little hope of being beautiful.

In the House of Lords in May 1985 Lord Melchett, East Anglian farmer, outspoken conservationist and opposition spokesman on the environment, said simply 'my heart lies in seeing a future where agriculture and conservation interests work much more closely together, where those interests are fully integrated, and where we are concerned not just with particular sites like SSSIs, but with what happens to the whole of the countryside'. Real integration will mean new kinds of policies for economic activities in the countryside which put livelihoods and the environment far higher on the agenda, above output and profitability. By any reckoning nature conservation will have an important role to play in the British countryside in the future. New policies are needed, and can be found. Much depends on them, and their success.

Chapter One

The changing countryside

The ratchet of change

In January 1981, debate over the Wildlife and Countryside Bill was at its height in Parliament. The Bill was supposed to be the most thorough treatment of conservation and the countryside for many years, and among other things it was hoped that it would guarantee the survival of the last vestigial patches of semi-natural habitat in Britain. Controversy over the proposals was already fierce. How serious a problem was habitat loss? How destructive was modern intensive agriculture? How should farmers, and others, be prevented from damaging wildlife sites? In the middle of all this, an article appeared in *New Scientist* written by David Goode, who was the deputy chief scientist of the Nature Conservancy Council, the government body responsible for nature conservation. Called 'the threat to wildlife habitats', the article explained quite simply that the Bill as it stood was not going to be strong enough to stop habitat loss.

Coming from such a source and at such a time, this article opened up the debate on habitat loss, and incidentally is rumoured to have won the NCC a sharp rap across the knuckles from the government for being too free with its opinions. The course of the debate, and the effect of the legislation eventually passed, are described later in this book. The figures presented by David Goode in his article showed that the most important areas for wildlife in Britain, scheduled as SSSIs, were being destroyed or degraded at a rate of 100 per year, more in some areas. In all habitats, chalk grassland, heathland, ancient woodland or wet-lands, the story of shrinkage and fragmentation was the same. These figures themselves were confirmed in 1984 when the NCC published *Nature conservation in Great Britain*, which summa-rised information on the destruction of natural and semi-natural habitats in Britain since the war. By 1984, 95% of lowland grasslands and herb-rich hay meadows lacked any significant wildlife interest, and only 3% were unaffected by agricultural improvement (Fig. 1.1). Eighty per cent of lowland chalk and limestone grasslands had been significantly damaged by agri-cultural 'reclamation' or the ending of former grazing regimes. Forty per cent of lowland heathland had been destroyed, most by agricultural conversion, afforestation or building: the heaths of Breckland shrank from 9200 ha in 1950 to 4500 ha in 1980, and the Dorset heathland had been reduced from 10 000 ha to 5600 ha since 1960, while the remaining pieces were fragmented and small in extent, vulnerable to damage by fire.

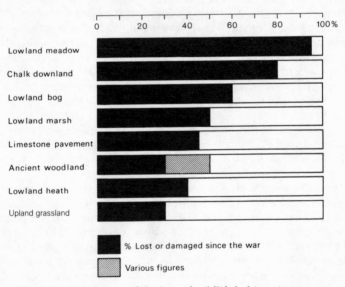

Figure 1.1 Estimates of the loss of wildlife habitats in postwar Britain.

2

Of limestone pavements in the North of England, 45% had been damaged or destroyed by 1984, largely by the gardening trade for rockery stone. Between 30 and 50% of ancient broadleaved woodland, (continuous on one site since AD 1600), in England and Wales had been lost since the war, mostly due to replanting with conifer species. Fenland drainage had reduced the area of fens in East Anglia from 10 000 to 1000 ha between 1930 and 1981. Sixty per cent of lowland raised mires had been damaged or destroyed by peat digging or afforestation since World War II, and 30% of upland bog, heath and grassland communities were lost between 1950 and 1980.

The forces in the countryside which caused these losses were by no means new. Similar activities had been transforming, and indeed creating, the countryside over the past 200 years. What caused such concern in the early 1980s was the scale and speed of change, and the tiny area of land rich in wildlife which had remained undeveloped. Many of the richest wildlife sites in Britain are those maintained by traditional forms of land husbandry. These include pastures which have not been ploughed up, treated with herbicide and artificial fertiliser and reseeded, old meadows still cut for hay and not silage, areas of downland or unimproved upland pasture, woodlands where deciduous trees are still grown, and upland ecosystems not planted with tracts of conifers. It is not man's use of the land which automatically destroys wildlife interest, but the form, and especially the intensity, of that use. Intensive afforestation and the relentless drive for greater output and efficiency in British agriculture have in their way been as effecitve in reducing the conservation interest of the countryside as the spread of industry and housing. However, they have affected a far larger area.

The conservationist today is in rather the same position as the farm labourer in the countryside of 200 years ago. He (or she) has few legal rights in the countryside, but has very real interests in the way the land is managed. He may no longer need grazing or fuelwood, but does need attractive landscapes and rich wildlife habitats. These are no less important products of the countryside than the farmers' crops, although they are less easily valued and sold. Modern agriculture and forestry have damaged those interests to an unprecedented extent, especially since World War II.

The representatives of farming organisations often like to argue that farmers are the original (and best) conservationists. This may be true in terms of agricultural resources (although there are many who would question the ecological sustainability of chemical farming techniques), but it has certainly not been true in terms of nature conservation in the past three decades. None the less, the image persists. A statement from a 1985 government paper responding to a Report of the House of Commons Select Committee on the Environment is typical, stating that 'most of what we now think of as the most attractive in the farmed landscape is the result of farmers responding to economic and technical pressures in the past'. Certainly it is true that change in the countryside has been brought about over a period of hundreds of years by individual farmers locked into an economic system which forced them to intensify production. Many farmers have found themselves caught in a high-input high-output treadmill. It is far less certain that this has been beneficial for farming (smaller farmers in particular have suffered), and certainly it has been damaging to the countryside and wildlife. Nicholas Bonsor MP said in a committee debate in the Commons in 1985 'When I look at the farming background in this country – and I declare my interest as a farmer – I see the enormous changes which have taken place since the war that have been wholly detrimental to the interests of conservation and the interests of agriculture and farming as a whole'.

Agriculture has moulded the countryside, and its own turbulent changes in fortune have had extensive repercussions in natural and semi-natural areas. Farmers are not conservationists: historically they are pawns and pieces on a turbulent chessboard. They have created a countryside as much by what it is unprofitable to do as by deliberate action.

Despite appearances in the past ten or twenty years, farmers have not always been prosperous. There have been periods of depression and bust in British agriculture, as well as booms. The fates of natural and semi-natural habitats in the countryside have been inextricably tied up with these swings in fortune: in the booms, agriculture has expanded onto new land and intensified, and semi-natural habitats have been lost; in the depressions land

4

has been fallowed. But these changes have not balanced each other out over time. Abandoned agricultural land does not suddenly regain its wildlife interest. Many ecosystems take many decades or even centuries to recover. There has been a ratchet at work, so that each progressive change involves further environmental transformation. Under the pressure of agricultural change, the countryside has become less attractive, less diverse in ecological terms, and (because both technological improvements and depressions caused farmers to sack labourers or not replace them), less lived in. As more demands have been made for recreation and access to the countryside by town dwellers, and increasingly for an agricultural landscape rich in wildlife, the countryside has become progressively less able to meet them. Former states are irrecoverable: the ratchet has turned, the pawl clicked home. The changes which have occurred seem to be more or less irreversible.

Of course, the relative wealth and leisure which allows us to want the intangible goods from the countryside – like the chance to see wild plants and animals – cannot be completely separated from the destruction of the countryside itself in the name of progress. There is a bitter irony here, but no inconsistency. We may all have benefited to some extent from the transformation of the countryside, and we have certainly increasingly encouraged the government to fund its destruction, but that does not make the desire to halt the damage invalid. Indeed, the dependence of the agricultural industry on subsidies paid by an overwhelmingly urban population makes their claim for a say in the way the land is used entirely appropriate. Food production is increasingly being seen as just another economic activity, not some sacred duty, and the urban taxpayer seems to be increasingly of the opinion that he who pays the piper should be allowed to call the tune. It is not illogical to want to reverse the trend of intensification in countryside land use, and that is what the conservation movement is currently trying to do. This book is about the simple question: how can the loss of wildlife habitat be stopped? But before tackling that we must examine the pattern of past changes in the countryside in more detail.

Improving the countryside

In 1848, 180 years of government protection for grain farmers ended when the Corn Laws were finally repealed. Despite the dire predictions of landowners, corn prices remained high for the next two decades, and between 1850 and 1870 farm incomes doubled, farm rents rose by a fifth, and rural labourers' wages began slowly to increase. Most farmers were tenants, but the real profits lay with land ownership. Landholding was excessively concentrated. A survey in 1873 claimed that there were a million landowners in England and Wales, but of these 0.7 million held less than one acre (0.4 ha). Just 1700 large landowners held over 14 million acres (5.6 million ha) between them.

The British population had doubled from the beginning of the 19th century to almost 21 million people by 1850, and it continued to rise. In 1850 almost half the population still lived and worked in the countryside. Although agricultural output increased through the 19th century (rising by between 50 and 80% between 1830 and 1880, for example), from the mid-century onwards the agricultural workforce began to decline in absolute numbers for the first time ever as machinery supplanted hand labour. The industrial population in urban areas rose rapidly.

The previous two centuries had seen fundamental and far-reaching changes in agriculture and the British countryside. Many innovations such as new fodder crops and crop rotations were introduced. Most had little or no distinguishable direct effect on wildlife. The improved methods still allowed a wide variety of species to coexist within the farmed landscape on fallowed land, rough grazings and woods, while substantial areas of undeveloped wild land remained in many parts of Britain. However, one development which did have a considerable effect was the enclosure movement.

From the middle of the 18th century, the old open field system in which different landholders held scattered strips of land in large fields gave way in lowland England to an enclosed landscape. Enclosure, which allowed each landowner to have his land in a single block, made the intensification of production much easier and more rewarding. Slowly at first, and then over extensive areas, larger landowners sought Acts of Parliament to enclose fields and common land. By 1793 over 1600 Acts of Enclosure had been made, covering a total of over 1 million ha. By 1815 a further 1970 Acts accounted for an additional 1.2 million ha, almost 17% of England. By 1830 a further 15 000 ha had been enclosed.

About the only gain from enclosures in terms of conservation was the establishment of great lengths of boundary hedge in the previously open-field counties of eastern England. These have become important as wildlife habitats only in recent years as small copses and woodlands have disappeared from the landscape. Against this has to be set the loss of extensive areas of semi-natural vegetation, and the increasingly intensive management of the enclosed land.

Enclosure had significant effects on many areas of semi-natural vegetation in the countryside which were held under common rights. Of the 2.3 million ha enclosed by 1830, 0.7 million ha was defined as 'common' or 'waste' land. Fully a third of the Acts of Enclosure involved waste. Whereas open field enclosure was concentrated in the Midland counties, enclosure of commons was more scattered. Thus over 20% of the counties of Cumberland and Westmorland were enclosed 'waste', and there were significant areas in Northumberland, Durham, Yorkshire and Somerset. On Exmoor, a man called John Knight enclosed 9000 ha under a single Act in 1817. A total of 18 000 ha had been enclosed by 1859.

In the 100 years prior to 1880 between 1.5 and 2.4 million ha of waste was enclosed, and much of it reclaimed. Most of this area would now be regarded as important wildlife habitat, but in the late 18th century the prevailing view was that of the agricultural improver Arthur Young, who asked rhetorically 'what say they to the improvement of moors in the northern counties, where enclosures alone have made these counties smile with culture which before were dreary as night?'. Few influential voices were raised against the enclosures, or against the loss of 'waste'. In the years of 'high farming' of the first three quarters of the 19th century enclosure and improvement continued steadily. Figure 1.2 shows the extent of such enclosure across England, based on the work of Michael Turner on Parliamentary enclosure.

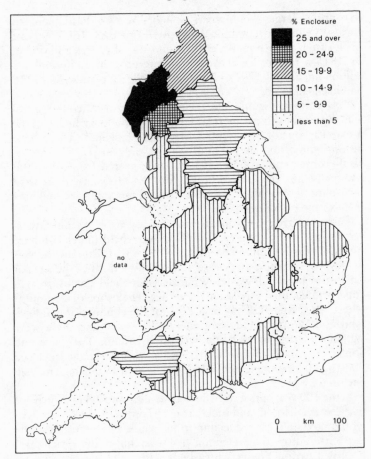

Figure 1.2 The enclosure of commons and wastes in England
1750–1830.

Fenlands were also widely transformed by agricultural
improvement. In East Anglia, the first steam pump was introduced at Littleport near Ely in 1819, and fen drainage proceeded
apace, perhaps the best-known single enterprise being the drainage of Whittlesey Mere in 1851. This was the last extensive piece

of open water left in the fenland, and it was the last known location where the now extinct British race of the large copper butterfly was recorded. Similar drainage work was done in Somerset, where almost 14% of the county was enclosed in the 18th and 19th centuries, a total of 59 000 ha. Acts to drain parts of the Somerset Levels were first passed in 1719 and 1721, and by 1859, 62 Acts accounted for 24 000 ha enclosed and drained.

In 1848, the government announced that it would give loans at low rates of interest for land drainage. The concern here was not the drainage of fenland (although this continued), but the under-drainage of heavy clay soils to make ploughing and arable cultivation possible. The £2 million allocated was exhausted almost at once, as was a further £2 million voted in 1850. By 1864, a total of £8 million had been spent by the Treasury and private investors on land drainage. The figure rose to £12 million by 1878 under the Land Drainage Act of 1861 and the Land Improvement Act of 1864. The ecological impact of this drainage was considerable. The decline of wet meadow butterfly species such as the marsh fritillary began at this period.

However, improvement was not always easy, and some other areas of the country proved more intractable. The Bagshot Heaths in Surrey (still surviving, although much degraded and fragmented) needed to be fertilised with horse manure, and deep ploughed to break up iron pans. It was costly and unremunerative work, and some at least of the enclosed land was left undeve-loped: an area of 1600 ha enclosed at Windlesham in 1814 was still largely heath, plus a few planted pines, in 1860. Many pieces of enclosed hill land were also left undeveloped. 22 000 ha were enclosed on the North Yorkshire Moors between 1748 and 1862, some in large stretches of 2000–3000 ha, but initial reclamation efforts were often abandoned. Thus at Kilburn, 425 ha were enclosed in 1828 and fenced, and by 1878 63% was arable or improved meadow and only 31% left as moor or rough pasture. Twelve years later the area of meadow land had fallen by 26%, as indeed it continued to do up to the 1950s, when only 25% was of improved standard.

The pattern of enclosure varied enormously across Britain, and much remains to be understood about its implications for the loss of natural and semi-natural habitats. What is quite clear is that

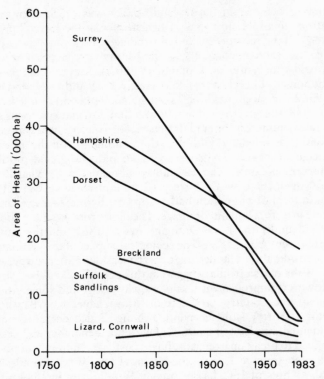

Figure 1.3 The loss of lowland heathland in England since 1750.

this phase of agricultural improvement brought about significant changes in the status of wildlife habitats. Figure 1.3 shows the decline in the area of lowland heath in Britain since 1750. In every area except the Lizard in Cornwall, heathland has been lost in each decade in the past two centuries. In the early part of this century urban growth was to blame in many areas (especially Surrey and Dorset), but the main factor in the 19th century, and indeed in the last 30 years, has been agricultural improvement. Thomas Hardy wrote about the wastes of Egdon Heath in Dorset towards the end of the last century, but the landscape he described was that of 50 years before. By the time he wrote the

10

heath was going, and now Dorset would be almost unrecognisable; indeed the recent film *Tess* had to be made in Brittany for lack of suitable locations in Britain.

The 'improvement' movement, was by no means confined to England. Its effects were striking and draconian in the Scottish Highlands, where the late 18th and early 19th centuries saw the clearance of small tenant farming communities, and their replacement with extensive sheep farms, and later shooting estates. It is the social impact of this black history which is best known, sympathetically chronicled, for example, by John Prebble in his book *The clearances*, but the implications of these changes both directly on grazing ecology and indirectly as a factor underlying current land use conflicts, are considerable.

Many developments occurred in 'the science of agriculture' through the 19th century. The first agricultural society (the Bath and West) was founded in 1777. By 1835 there were 100 local agricultural societies, and the number rose to 700 by 1875. The Royal Agricultural Society of England (RASE) was founded in 1838 (Scotland, as so often, being ahead: the Highland and Agricultural Society of Scotland was founded in 1784). The RASE Annual Show began in 1840, and was soon attracting crowds of over 100 000. New machinery such as the steam plough, steam barn engines and theshers as well as all kinds of horse-drawn implements including reapers and metal ploughs were demonstrated. Even the disastrously wet show at Kilburn in 1879 attracted 187 000 visitors, and had almost 12 000 exhibits. By 1870 knowledge of 'agricultural chemistry' (i.e. organic chemistry) had grown. Leibig's book *Chemistry and its application to agriculture and physiology* was published in translation in 1840, and the use of fertilisers developed from the rather *ad hoc* use of bone meal on vegetables to the manufacture of superphosphates. By the 1850s Chilean nitrate and Peruvian phosphate fertilisers were being imported in large quantities. Manufactured agricultural feeds were introduced in the 1840s, and as their use expanded pasture was turned over to arable cropping.

There were new ideas in forestry by the mid-19th century also. Oak for shipbuilding continued to dominate British forestry after the end of the French wars, although woodland owners started to experiment with shorter rotations and hence quicker returns on investment. Through the century, coppice management became more regularised and intensive, and enthusiasm for new plantations, especially of exotic species, grew. The Royal Society of Arts gave awards for tree planting from 1758 onwards, and the practice of planting conifers started slowly to spread. For example, almost 2 million trees were planted in 1820 on the Duke of Devonshire's estate in Cumberland, 1 million of them larch. By the end of the 18th century Norway spruce, silver fir, European larch and Corsican pine had been introduced to Britain. By 1854 the Douglas fir, sitka spruce and lodgepole pine (among many others) had been added. They began to appear in an increasing number of plantations as the century wore on.

The countryside in decline

In 1870 the total arable area in England was 5 million ha, of which 1.3 million ha was wheat. However, cheap grain imported from America and meat brought in new refrigerated ships from Argentina and Australia were beginning to cause food prices to fall. Despite a series of bad harvests in the early 1870s and early 1880s, which might have been expected to push grain prices up, they in fact fell by 50% between 1870 and 1890.

Land started to go out of arable production, at first newly reclaimed land and that on the upland margin and heavy lowland clays, then more generally: between 1875 and 1885 in the arable districts of England the arable area fell by 200 000 ha, the area under wheat from 0.73 to 0.64 million ha. In the next decade there was a further 0.2 million ha decline in arable land, and wheat acreage fell to under 0.4 million ha. There was acute distress in the previously wealthy arable counties as the profitable world of high farming came to pieces. In other sectors, things were less bleak. Livestock farmers did rather better because of cheap foodgrains, and dairying and market gardening expanded to supply the growing urban markets. Vacant tenancies in once wealthy arable Essex were taken up by Scottish livestock farmers and run profitably on a low-input low-output system.

The response of most farmers to this crisis was either to move out of arable production as far as they could, or to further reduce costs. Mechanisation was important here because it reduced labour requirements, and agricultural wages had risen in the 1870s with the short-lived rise of Joseph Arch's National Agricultural Labourers Union (this grew to 70 000 members in a year, but declined after a successful lockout by farmers in East Anglia in 1874). Labour costs were also reduced by accepting a lower level of husbandry, and many fields grew weedy crops in the last quarter of the century. The productivity of labour rose by 70% between 1840 and 1900, partly due to the use of horse-drawn machinery. The number of horses rose from 1.3 million in 1811 and only 2.1 million in 1871 to an all-time peak of 3.3 million in 1901. However, the rural labour force declined. By 1901 less than 1.3 million were employed on the land, a mere 12% of the working population of the country.

By 1914, the area under arable agriculture was as small as at any time for decades: in total 4.4 million ha, of which only 0.73 million ha was wheat, while fully 6.5 million ha was permanent grass. Two thirds of British farm output comprised either livestock or feed for livestock. In the 1911 census, 0.23 million people claimed to be 'farmers' or 'graziers' out of a total of 1.35 million people working on the land. Those farmers, most of them still tenants, who had access to land and the capital to farm it formed the National Farmers' Union (NFU) in 1908 (initially called the Lincolnshire Farmers' Union). This excluded landowners (already well-enough represented at Westminster) and stood against a new labourers union, the National Agricultural Labourers Union, established two years later in Norfolk.

Almost half a million hectares of land went out of arable cropping between 1870 and 1914, and a larger area was being cropped less intensively, managed as permanent pasture, or lying fallow. It is likely that some wild animal and plant species profited by this depressed state of agriculture, but in fact the balance of gains and losses is by no means clear. Reclaimed land on the upland margin, for example, which was abandoned at this period has still (almost a century later) not redeveloped its original dwarf shrub vegetation of heather and bilberry. A series of case studies made by the Institute of Terrestrial Ecology (ITE) show that only half of the pastures abandoned by 1905 had reverted to grassy heaths by the 1980s, and shrub heath commu-

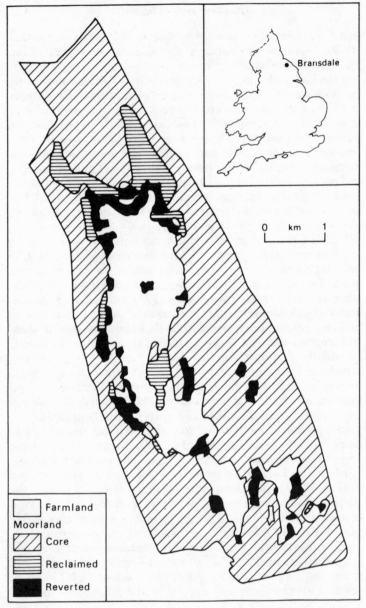

Figure 1.4 Change in moorland habitats in one parish in the North Yorks Moors, showing areas converted to farming and areas which have gone back to moorland in the period since 1850.

nities were only slowly developing on land abandoned around 1850. Figure 1.4 shows data from the parish of Bransdale in the North York Moors. Although most of the moorland and farmland has remained unaltered, there is a substantial marginal area which has either been converted from moorland relatively recently, or has been farmland at some stage since 1850 and has now reverted to moorland. The conservation interest of these reverted areas will be reduced, as will that of areas currently reclaimed. The total turnover of moorland is considerable. Because, in the 1980s, we equate agricultural development with the loss of wildlife interest in land, it is tempting to assume that agricultural decay would reverse the process. Then, as indeed now, this was rarely the case. Despite the agricultural decline, the losses to wildlife habitats of the previous century were not reversed.

Over the same period in which these changes in agriculture were taking place, the urban and industrial population was growing enormously. Towns began to sprawl out into the countryside which their working people had so recently left. The rural population of England fell by between 0.65 and 0.85 million people every decade from 1841 onwards. London suburbs like Willesden and Tottenham and their equivalents in Manchester, Birmingham and other cities doubled and redoubled their population. Expanding railway systems, and after the turn of the century the rise of the motorised bus and to a lesser extent the motor cycle and the car, killed the old coaching routes, but also ended the isolation of the countryside. Socially, economically and politically the countryside had ceased to be central to national life by the turn of the century. Although the agricultural depression had temporarily ended the loss of wildlife habitats in the name of agricultural improvement, pressure on the countryside continued in the form of urban expansion.

The end of the 19th century also saw the flowering of the shooting estate. Sport shooting had expanded following the invention of the percussion cap in 1820. As the century wore on, many woodlands in the English lowlands were turned over to pheasant rearing, and in the uplands sheep gave way to grouse. In Scotland, deer stalking became high fashion, and dominated many estates, throwing into stark relief the failure of the kelp industry in the Outer Isles (burned for phosphate fertiliser, and killed off by South American fertiliser imports) and the resulting destitution of the few communities to have survived the earlier clearances. For wildlife, if not for people, game management was fairly beneficial, except in the ruthless eradication of supposed predators. The red kite and hen harrier were persecuted to the edge of extinction in the 19th century, as were birds of prey like the peregrine, buzzard and golden eagle as well as the wildcat and the pine marten. There are no firm figures, of course, but the impact on predator populations was considerable. With the pressures of egg collecting and taxidermy, other hobbies of 'gentlemen', raptors in particular had a hard time. Both the sea eagle and the osprey became extinct through over-collecting.

The importance of game rearing on large estates was enhanced by the virtual abandonment by the Royal Navy of timber-built ships after the 1880s. The lessons of engagements between 'ironclads' and wooden vessels in the American Civil War were learned quickly, and while the navy turned to steam power, woodland owners either let their gamekeepers take over, or listened to the newly founded English Arboricultural Society (now the Royal Forestry Society), and planted conifers. Forestry had been at a low ebb for at least a century. Suddenly a range of bodies expressed a concern, the RASE (who included a forestry exhibit in their 1904 show) and even the University of Cambridge, who appointed a Reader in Forestry in 1907. In 1909 the Royal Commission on Coast Erosion and Afforestation reported that as much as 9 million acres of Britain might be suitable for trees, and in 1912 the Board of Agriculture Advisory Committee recommended a two-phase survey of Britain to determine the most suitable areas for afforestation, and the establishment of a 5000 acre 'experimental forest'. Nothing was done. In 1914, Ray Lankester wrote in *Nature* 'in this country we have no department of forestry, no knowledge or practice of forestry, and we shall very soon have no forests'.

The 1914–18 war changed the picture. By its end, the government had become deeply involved not only in forestry, but also in agriculture. Food supplies were seen to be but a small problem in 1914, although in fact the country had only a few months supply of bread corn and wheat. Almost at once, however, farms began to lose skilled men and farm horses to the army in France. Almost a sixth of farm labourers had been signed up by the middle of 1915. Also, the supply of imported grain and fertiliser was severely curtailed by the war at sea, and prices rose. By June 1916 they were 60% above pre-war levels.

A government report in May 1915 recommended drastic steps. The government should fix a price for corn for three years to guarantee farmers' profits in order to persuade them to bring some 2–3 million acres of land which had reverted to pasture back into cultivation. It was in this year that N. C. Rothschild's Society for the Promotion of Nature Reserves (SPNR) sent a list of sites of importance for nature conservation to the Board of Agriculture, in the hope that these could be spared the plough.

In fact the government did not accept guaranteed prices until February 1917, when the prices of wheat and oats were fixed for six years (not barley, out of deference to the temperance movement), and county agricultural committees were established to oversee the expansion of agricultural production. The Corn Production Bill 1917 allowed for a deficiency payment per acre on the fall of the average market price below a set minimum.

With this support, arable cropping expanded from 4.5 million ha in 1916 (just above the 1914–15 figure) to 4.6 million ha in 1917 and then more sharply to 5 million ha in 1918. Because of the need to fallow land which had been under wheat the previous two years, the 1918 figure required the ploughing of 0.8 million ha of permanent grass and 200 000 ha of temporary grass. Labour was short, so this ploughing was not spread equally round the country, but was concentrated in the South and East where machinery was more plentiful (especially the old-fashioned steam plough sets) and the targets could most easily be met. The losses of permanent pasture were therefore greatest in just those counties where the most land was already under the plough. Lowland woodlands also suffered at this time. Under the Home Grown Timber Committee, and later the Timber Supply Department of the Board of Trade, some 0.45 million acres of woodland was felled, most of it old broadleaved woodland, and much of it oak. Among the areas cleared was Monks Wood in Huntingdonshire. This was allowed to regenerate and is now in fact a National Nature Reserve (NNR), largely because it is the only one

17

of the many woods in the area to have escaped subsequent more permanent clearance.

Between two wars

World War I stimulated considerable thought about the proper place of government involvement in both forestry and agriculture. In 1916, the Forestry Sub-committee of the Ministry of Reconstruction, chaired by F. D. Acland MP, wrote the blueprint for today's Forestry Commission (FC). This made a bold proposal that the government should establish a forest authority able to acquire land and disburse grants to private owners. This should plant over 0.72 million ha with trees (calculated to give a three year strategic reserve of timber), planting 80 000 ha in the first decade. Despite the misgivings of the Treasury official on the Acland committee, the times were such that the Forestry Act 1919 was passed with great alacrity by Parliament (in one month and 10 days). The FC was duly established, with a budget of £3.5 million. The first trees were planted in Devon before the end of the year, 19 000 ha were acquired in the first year, and some 700 ha planted. In 1921 the Geddes committee on National Expenditure recommended that the young FC should be scrapped, but it was saved (although severely reduced) by some rapid and effective lobbying of Cabinet and Parliament by its first chairman, Lord Lovat, and it continued to expand and plant trees through the 1920s. Claims that forestry could generate employment in depressed areas won it some reprieve on budget cuts on several occasions. By 1929 it had planted 56 000 ha, almost all with conifers.

Agriculture's progress was less happy. The Selborne Committee on postwar agricultural policy reported in January 1917, recommending the extension of guaranteed prices for farmers and reasonable wages for farm workers. In 1919, a Royal Commission produced a majority report which followed a similar line, and two dissenting views. In the event guaranteed cereal prices were incorporated into the Agriculture Act 1920. County and District Agriculture Executive Committees were continued, and the Land Drainage Act 1918 allowed the formation of drainage boards.

18

Farm profits had been high through the war, but rents remained low, and many landowners sold farms to their tenants. One quarter of England changed hands between 1918 and 1921, the biggest shift in ownership since the dissolution of the monasteries under Henry VIII. The NFU grew, and by 1921 had 80 000 members in 58 county branches. However, all was not rosy. Much arable land was exhausted by continuous cropping during the war, and had to be fallowed to get it back into rotation. Food prices rose after the war, but then collapsed in 1921, heralding a new and deeper depression for agriculture. The government foresaw a huge bill if they paid the guaranteed prices set by the 1920 Act, and hastily repealed parts of it, paying only £19.7 million in 1922 to cover land already planted. Farmers, particularly those owner–occupiers who had taken out mortgages, fell into debt, and a number went broke. Agricultural wages fell, while the length of the labourer's working week rose. At the same time, unemployment nationally was rising rapidly (topping 1 million in 1923).

Although the British Sugar (Subsidy) Act 1925 promoted the expansion of sugar beet in the East of England, the arable acreage in England as a whole declined through the 1920s, falling from 4.8 million ha in 1920 to under 4 million ha in 1929. Low capital inputs, low incomes and indebtedness dogged arable farming, although low grain prices favoured livestock and milk production, and market gardening expanded.

The interwar period was, of course, one of almost uncontrolled urban expansion. Early town planning Acts were more concerned with the building of housing of acceptable quality than with controlling sprawl. The word 'suburb' in the 1930s implied a healthy and attractive place to live, and had few of its modern more derogatory connotations. Some 4 million houses were built between the wars. At the end of the 1920s and the early 1930s, about 17 000 ha of land was being used for house construction every year, and the figure rose to over 20 000 ha a year between 1934 and 1939. The total loss of agricultural land between 1927 and 1934 to all uses (housing, sports, war office) was 0.3 million ha.

At this time of agricultural depression urban development was perceived as more of a significant threat to the countryside than

19

agriculture. Thus, for example, lists of possible nature reserves drawn up in the early 1940s speak of damaging building development on the North Downs between Box Hill and Reigate in Surrey, and on the sandy heaths near Frensham Ponds. Golf courses or hotels threatened coastal areas, including Dawlish Warren and Braunton Burrows in Devon, Hengistbury Head near Bournemouth, and the Wallasey Sandhills in Cheshire. None the less, forestry and agriculture were not without damaging impact. Brickhill Heath in Buckinghamshire, for example, was reported to have been 'spoiled' by afforestation, as was part of Wareham Heath in Dorset, while on Fleam Dyke in Cambridgeshire an area of pasque flower was destroyed by a farmer 'as he disliked people frequenting the spot'.

In the 1930s the crisis of agriculture deepened. Prices of both grain and livestock collapsed in 1931 and 1932. Initially the Labour government, trapped by the need to keep food prices low, could do little. However, the new National Government introduced price guarantees again in the Wheat Act of 1932. This halted, but did not reverse, the decline of arable cropping, at about 3.7 million ha. Marketing boards were also established for various commodities (milk in 1933, potatoes in 1934) and there was some protection against imports in these commodities. The government's immediate concern was to return to the situation in agriculture of 1927–9, and although the NFU maintained pressure for a positive long-term policy for agriculture and a substantially higher standard of living for farmers across the whole country (and not just the wheat and sugar farms of the East) this was not achieved.

Once again, the arable counties bore the brunt of the difficulties. The countryside was deeply depressed economically, but in places its value for wildlife was enhanced. Many acres returned to unhusbanded use for the first time since their improvement in the 19th century, and some developed high wildlife value quite quickly. Edith Whetham, author of the *Cambridge history of agriculture* for this period, describes the impact of this dereliction. 'There were thousands of acres of waterlogged marshes in Essex and Suffolk beloved of wildfowlers and shooting parties, acres which had grown wheat, beef and mutton up to 1920, but then fell derelict as sea banks were breached by winter gales and not repaired, dykes were no longer cleaned out, and the livestock were sold to pay debts, not to buy their replacements. The country was unkempt, with overgrown hedges, choked drains and ditches, abandoned fields, derelict steadings and condemned cottages tumbling into ruin. The millions of acres of unproductive pasture which eased the way of the travellers, and which provided cover for foxes, rabbits, pheasants, wild duck and marsh birds, were a depressing witness to the loss of income, of capital and of hope, inflicted by twenty years of remorseless deflation in the farming communities of England and Wales'.

Of course, some farmers went bankrupt at this period, although not a vast number considering the depth of the depression nationally in other businesses. Two thousand six hundred farmers became bankrupt between 1930 and 1936, but equally some agri-businessmen such as 'the carrot king', Arthur Rickwood, with access to large holdings on good soils, did extremely well. Furthermore, although the arable acreage in England overall continued to fall (in 1939 it was lower than at any time since the previous war), overall productivity increased. Partly this was due to the further decline in the numbers of people employed on the land. The number of horses also fell, there were probably less than half a million farm horses by the mid-1930s, while the number of tractors, mechanical harvesters and milking machines grew. With the passing of the horse as the basis of agricultural traction, the era of mixed farming began to end, and the patterns of mechanisation we know in agriculture today began to develop. The Agriculture Act 1937 subsidised artificial fertiliser, especially for use on grasslands. Official agricultural advice began to stress its use to raise productivity, as did the work of the Agricultural Research Council, founded in 1931. Interestingly, this period saw the origins of the ideas of organic farming in reaction to these new trends.

Discussions about agriculture in the event of war began as early as 1936, when the Food (Defence Plans) Department was set up in the Board of Trade. Both farmers and civil servants were determined to avoid the disasters of the previous war. In 1939 the Agricultural Development Act was passed, which backed once again the expansion of agricultural production. Subsidies of £2 per acre were payable for ploughing grassland over seven years

21

old, and a sheep subsidy was also among the incentives to increased production offered. Farmers were being asked once again to feed the nation in time of war. It was a challenge they were to rise to vigorously, as indeed they had done in 1917 and 1918. This time they were able to keep the government assistance so gained into the peace which followed. In time they were able to build very substantially upon it.

Postwar policy

World War II marked a turning point in the fortunes of both agriculture and forestry. The policies developed during the war, based on the intensification and expansion of agriculture under protection from imports, and of continued afforestation, have had a major effect on almost all natural and semi-natural habitats in the countryside. As John Bowers, economist and uncompromising commentator on agricultural policy, acidly puts it, 'by any standards, British farmers had a good war'.

Within hours of the declaration of war on 3 September 1939, the Ministry of Agriculture had established new War Agriculture Executive Committees in each county of England and Wales (many of them run by NFU branch chairmen) to oversee the putting of grassland to the plough. The target was an extra 0.6 million ha of crops in 1940. The committees had powers under the defence regulations to requisition land or farm machinery, to direct how farmland and sporting or recreation areas should be managed, and to terminate tenancies. Between 1940 and 1948 they took possession of 152 000 ha on the grounds of bad husbandry, two thirds of it through terminated tenancies (almost 3000 in number).

The results were impressive, if undesirable from the point of view of nature conservation. An extra 1.5 million ha was tilled in 1939 and 1940. The area of tillage rose from 3.6 million ha in 1939 to 5.5 million ha in 1942, and stayed at that level until the end of the war. Somewhat ironically, this was more than equalled by the area taken out of agriculture for military purposes, especially airfields. Figure 1.5 shows the shift in the area of arable over the period of the war. Extensive areas of grassland were

22

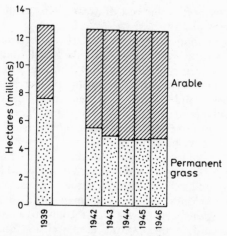

Figure 1.5 Changes in the area of crops and grass in Great Britain and Northern Ireland 1939–46.

ploughed for the first time for generations, including among many other areas large parts of chalk grassland on the South Downs sheepwalks. These have remained under the plough ever since. There was also considerable wetland reclamation. As Anthony Hurd, appointed in 1939 to a senior advisory post in the Ministry of Agriculture, commented in his book *A farmer in Whitehall*, 'Every county can show records of good work done during the war in rescuing successful farmland from oblivion'.

Among these 'rescues' was the reclamation of 2400 ha of Hockwold and Feltwell Fens in southwest Norfolk which had been 'derelict' and flooded since a river embankment had broken in 1913. The fen was surveyed in 1940, then pumped dry and ploughed. About 400 ha were put down to crops, despite shrinkage of the peat and frost problems. Other extensive reclamation schemes were carried out in the Montgomeryshire hills, where over 400 ha was ploughed up for potatoes, and the Savernake Forest in Wiltshire. Here 200 ha of rough parkland was burned, deep ploughed and fertilised for the first time since at least the 16th century. Some County Executive Committees sought advice

23

on the conservation interest of areas proposed for reclamation, but by no means all.

These reclamations were particularly important as an example to farmers in nearby areas. Anthony Hurd commented of the Savernake Forest that 'the practical demonstration which Savernake provided as a ways and means of increasing production from derelict land proved a great encouragement to farmers to tackle similar land in their own occupation. Indeed, thousands of acres were brought under cultivation more quickly and efficiently than would have been the case had not Savernake been cleared'. Another area of land ploughed for the first time for centuries was Malmesbury Common in Wiltshire. Of this area Hurd comments 'The common has been returned to the burgesses of Malmesbury to whom it belongs, although they made little use of it before the war. Wisely, the burgesses have let the land to a farmer who, I am glad to record, is farming the land well. So another piece of England has, we may hope, been added permanently to the country's cultivated area'. Many 'pieces of England', and of Wales and Scotland, were ploughed up in the 1940s, and most have remained in intensive use. The ploughing was done at a time of overriding national need, and that need was met, but at a cost in terms of habitat loss that we are only now coming to appreciate.

Gross agricultural output in money terms increased by about three times during the war, although this partly simply reflects price rises. The need to fallow the newly cultivated land from 1943 was compensated for by higher yields due to the use of fertilisers and mechanisation. Wheat output rose by two thirds, oats (for animal feeds, whose importation was reduced greatly) by three quarters, and the production of potatoes doubled. It was an impressive performance, more than matching that in other industries. The Minister of Agriculture said in 1944 'I know of no industry that in this war has so resolutely pulled itself up by the roots and revolutionised its output and practice'. Anthony Hurd commented a few years later 'wherever we farmed, we could all feel pleased and proud that British agriculture was answering effectively the call for increased production ... there was real joy and satisfaction in winning food from the many thousands of acres that had lain almost unused in the inter-war years'.

Timber supplies were also the focus of much attention during the war. The Forestry Commission (FC) was split in 1939 into a timber production department (later incorporated into the Ministry of Supply) and a forest management department. There were powers to ensure the proper management of private forests, in the form of the compulsory purchase of standing timber. Twenty-seven out of 806 purchases in Wales were of this kind. Between 1939 and 1944, over 10 000 ha of FC forest was felled, 11 000 ha planted, and a further 70 000 ha acquired. Most of the timber felled, however, was the old, and largely private broadleaved woodlands. Some 196 000 ha of private forest were felled between 1939 and 1949.

The FC made its case for continued government support after the war in 1943, in a document entitled *Post-war forestry policy*. This was described by George Ryle, who wrote the history of the FC up to 1967, as 'without doubt the greatest and most productive work the Forestry Commission has ever undertaken'. It was certainly timely, and well-received. It proposed a planting target of 2 million ha, of which 1.2 million ha was to comprise presently treeless land, and argued that the government should continue to support a forest authority to control the whole industry in Britain, and a forest service of qualified practical forestry expertise. The FC, of course, fulfilled both functions. It was suggested that 0.44 million ha should be planted in the first decade, for which £41.2 million was needed. This the FC was granted under the Forestry Acts of 1945 and 1947. At the same time the Commission was put under the aegis of the Ministry of Agriculture.

By September 1949, the FC estate was 0.63 million ha, of which 225 000 ha were planted. Private forestry also expanded after the war, profiting from the Dedication Scheme introduced in the 1947 Act and the Approved Estates scheme introduced in 1953. Land acquisition was something of a problem, and attempts to acquire it by compulsory purchase in places like the Towy Valley in Wales were extremely unpopular. None the less, the FC's holding rose. By 1959 it held almost 1 million ha, 28% of it in Scotland, although only half was planted.

The shape of postwar agriculture was also set before the end of the war, by extending the principles used in the war itself. The

Agriculture Act 1947 established an annual price review (carried out by the ministry in consultation with the NFU) and price guarantees on all major products based on deficiency payments to farmers to bring selling prices up to the fixed levels. In 1944 the Minister of Agriculture wrote 'I believe in a progressive agriculture, not only for the benefit of those engaged in it, but also as a potent factor in restoring prosperity to the nation'. The 1947 Act guaranteed that vision of a stable, prosperous and progressive agricultural industry.

The theme of postwar agricultural policy has been the increase of productivity. Rationing was lifted in stages, finally ending in 1955. As the costs of production rose, the ministry squeezed farmers into being more efficient by slowly reducing price guarantees and by adjusting the emphasis of government support from guaranteed prices to subsidies on agricultural chemicals and improvements to the land. However, this support system was costly, and by the end of the 1950s the ministry was announcing a halt to expansion, and it cut the prices of milk, wheat and sheep. In 1961 and 1963 it introduced quotas for barley, pigs and eggs.

This trend towards the restriction of growth in agricultural output was only temporary. The NFU held detailed discussions with the ministry in the early 1960s, and from 1964 imported food began to be controlled. This market protection opened the way to further substantial growth in output. It was a policy whose chief focus was the incomes of farmers, and it was accompanied by various other measures to make agriculture more 'efficient'. The 1965 White Paper *The development of agriculture* encouraged greater mechanisation, specialisation and the amalgamation of farms to make larger units. Increased output became even more important to the government in the early 1970s because it promised to reduce the cost of entry into the European Economic Community (EEC). Output per acre indeed rose rapidly, while the number of agricultural workers fell. The countryside was transformed once more by the needs of the increasingly industrial form of agricultural production.

The form of agricultural support changed on Britain's entry into the EEC in 1972. Guaranteed price payments gave way to intervention purchasing to maintain prices, but did not affect the general pressure towards increased intensification and production. In 1975 the White Paper *Food from our own resources* confirmed the wisdom of continuing to expand production, a policy maintained four years later in *Farming and the nation*. Farmers responded impressively: the proportion of homegrown temperate foodstuffs rose from 59% in 1970 to 75% in 1980. However, the wisdom and great cost of agricultural policy has been strongly criticised, most notably perhaps by the Conservative MP Richard Body. His two books *Agriculture: the triumph and the shame* (1982) and *Farming in the clouds* (1984) and his bulldog hustings style, have gained widespread attention. His figure of over £3000 million as the annual cost of agricultural support called into question the validity of existing agricultural policies.

John Bowers and Paul Cheshire in *Agriculture, the countryside and land use* (1983) complain that the claimed efficiency of agriculture is technical rather than economic. It depends on gadgets, high technology and plentiful fossil fuels. Continuing expansion of agricultural output helps Britain's overall EEC budgetary contribution, but adds to the cost of the common agricultural policy (CAP), a share of which Britain of course bears. Richard Body calculated in 1984 that the cost of price support for agriculture in Britain, adjusted to 1983/84 prices, rose from £1696 million in 1955–6 to £3150 million in 1982–3. Not without reason, John Bowers called in a paper in 1985 on postwar agricultural policy for an end to 'the wearying dash for growth in agricultural production we have been experiencing since the war'.

These agricultural policies have had significant effects on the industry itself. The area under tillage, having fallen somewhat at the end of the war, rose once more. It was 4.5 million ha in 1955, 4.9 million ha in 1969 and 5.2 million ha in 1984. With this has gone a dramatic rise in yields, which has had the single greatest effect on output. Average wheat yields rose from 2.1 tonnes per ha in 1945 (little more than at the turn of the century) to 5.9 tonnes per ha in 1980 and 7.6 tonnes in 1984.

This has been made possible largely by plant breeding, and by increasing the amount of fertiliser and pesticides applied to crops. Phosphorous fertiliser use rose rapidly from 0.17 million tonnes in 1939 to 0.45 million tonnes in 1950, then levelled off. The

27

usage of potassium fertiliser continued to rise until 1965 before levelling off (at about 430 000 tonnes). The usage of nitrogen continued to rise, increasing by 70% from 1970–79. Over 1 million tonnes were used in 1979. Pesticide use has also expanded tremendously. There were few pesticides available prior to 1950, but there has been rapid development of crop protection chemicals, and in pesticide sales, subsequently. By the 1950s 20 kinds of herbicides and 24 chemicals to kill variously insects, molluscs, nematodes and mites had been introduced. New chemicals continued to be introduced in subsequent decades, with a shift from organochlorine compounds (like DDT and Dieldrin) towards more toxic but less persistent organophosphorus pesticides, and there were also developments in herbicides for broadleaved and then grass weeds. In the 1960s and 1970s, a number of fungicidal sprays were developed, and used extensively.

High-technology farming left little room for the organisms that were once a natural part of the agricultural scene. Agricultural weeds like the corn cockle and the cornflower (Fig. 1.6) declined in weed-free fields and hedgeless landscapes, as did flowers like the burnt orchis with the loss of limestone grassland (Fig. 1.7). Some butterflies also declined, for example the marsh fritillary, silver-spotted skipper and chalkhill and adonis blues. Their decline and that of other butterfly species since the war is described in the excellent *Atlas of butterflies of Britain and Ireland* (1984). Many less well known invertebrates as well as songbirds, gamebirds and birds of prey suffered similar fates, becoming reduced in numbers or locally extinct.

Government policy also brought about a shift in the pattern of agriculture, with a big rise in cereal acreages. The area of barley increased by 2.4 times between 1955 and 1969, and although the area then fell, wheat in its turn began to expand. The area under wheat rose from 0.76 million ha in 1955 to 0.79 million ha in 1969 and 1.3 million ha in 1979. Cereals spread out of their old fastness in the East. By 1979 every county in England except Cumbria had at least 10% of its arable land under wheat or barley, while 60% of the old cereal counties was under 'king corn'. This shift to wheat and barley, and to a lesser extent other arable crops, has demanded extensive land drainage. The area

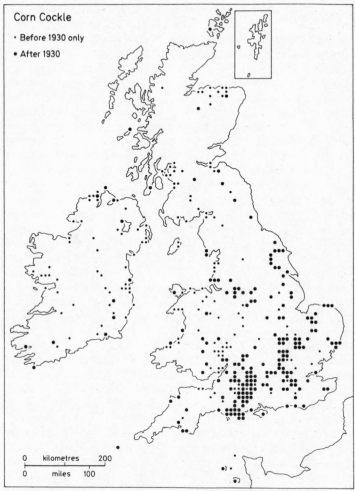

Figure 1.6 Changes in the distribution of the corn cockle.

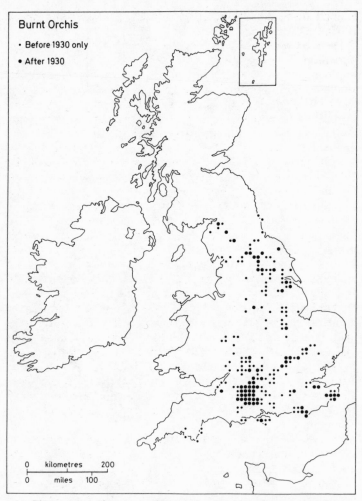

Figure 1.7 Changes in the distribution of the burnt orchis.

drained rose annually to 1970, subsequently levelling off at 100 000 ha per year.

There have been other important changes in the countryside. Agricultural mechanisation has continued to increase, and rural employment to decline. In 1950 the rural workforce was over half a million, but by the end of the 1970s it was less than half this figure. Working horses had virtually disappeared by the mid-1960s, and with them much of the incentive for mixed farming. Overall, farms have become larger, especially in England, and smaller farms less numerous. At the turn of the century there were 440 000 farmers in England and Wales, in the 1930s 400 000. By 1984 there were only 239 000 farm holdings recorded in the Annual Review of Agriculture. Prosperity and 'efficiency' did what depression could not, and pushed large numbers of farmers off the land. In 1955 only 3% of farms were over 300 acres. In 1973 the proportion was 8% and rising. The tendency towards owner-occupation which began in 1918 has also persisted. In 1950 7 million ha of England and Wales were rented and 4.4 million ha in owner-occupation. By 1973 the balance had altered, and only 5.2 million ha were rented. In 1984 60% of agricultural land in Britain was farmed by its owner. Also significant was the dramatic rise in the value of farmland over the 1970s, which made land a good investment. This brought financial institutions like pension funds as well as other business interests into farming. By 1974 1.3% of agricultural land in Britain was held by institutions, and the proportion continued to rise. Farm managers were appointed to serve the new owners, and more cold-blooded attitudes to the potential financial return on farmland became common.

By 1984 Ministry of Agriculture, Fisheries and Food (MAFF) statistics showed that there was a total of just over 7 million ha of arable land in Britain, 5.1 million ha of permanent grassland (at least five years old) and 6 million ha rough grazing. Both permanent grassland and rough pasture were declining slowly. Over half the arable acreage was down to barley (28% of the total) or wheat (28%). The agricultural industry still viewed the loss of arable land to urban uses as a major problem, but the urban area (which doubled between 1900 and 1950) was still only 11% of the country in 1971, and has risen relatively slowly

31

since. In the three decades after the end of the war the conversion of farmland was 15 700 ha per year, less than two thirds of the 1930s figure. As the late Robin Best of Wye College wrote in his book *Land use and living space*, 'in other words there is no real land problem in Britain at the moment. Most of the perceived problem is simply in the mind; it is not there on the ground'.

A bigger consumer of agricultural land in recent years has in fact been forestry, particularly in Scotland. Intensive forestry management has also expanded in the last 20 years, both on FC and private land, although policy has been less homogenous. The wartime concern with a strategic reserve of timber gave way in the early 1960s (the age of nuclear weapons) to an interest in other functions of forestry, including employment creation and recreation, as well as economics. None the less, planting continued. In 1965 the FC held 1.1 million ha, of which 0.6 million ha was planted, and in 1970 the area of Dedicated Woodland was 0.4 million ha. However, a policy review in 1972 cast doubt on the economic soundness of further large-scale planting, and a far more limited afforestation programme was proposed. The landscape and amenity function of forestry was stressed rather than any economic function.

This paper provoked prolonged and spirited criticism from private forestry organisations, as did the 1975 Finance Act which introduced Capital Transfer Tax. The rate of private planting fell in the late 1970s as a result to less than 10 000 ha per year, and at the same period the FC's own planting rate was reduced because agricultural subsidies on hill land made it too expensive. However, in 1977 the FC counter-attacked, and suggested raising the forested area in Britain to 1.8 million ha by the year 2025. An influential paper by the Centre for Agricultural Strategy in 1980 backed up this optimistic suggestion, and in the past few years the pendulum of policy has swung back strongly in favour of afforestation.

The area of afforested land in Britain has continued to grow, and is now slightly over 2 million ha. Of this, over half is in private ownership, and the vast majority consists of coniferous species in commercial plantations. Planting by private landowners had become brisk by 1984, with almost 20 000 ha planted (at a cost in FC grants of £5.8 million). Only 9% of this

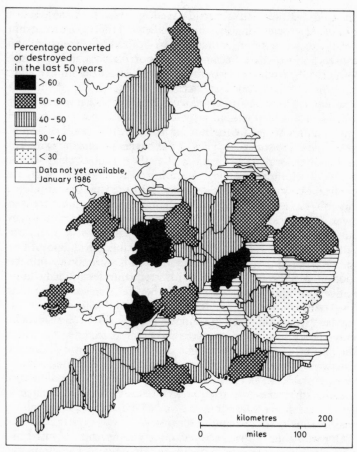

Figure 1.8 The loss of ancient semi-natural woodland in the past 50 years, in England and Wales.

planting was of native broadleaved species. In 1985 the FC published a review of policy for broadleaved timber growing, but it was greeted without enthusiasm by both private foresters and conservation owners because it did not do enough to reverse former policy which discouraged broadleaved planting. Figure 1.8 shows data on the decline in the area of ancient woodland which has occurred since the war as a result of these policies. Data of this kind are being collated on all counties in England and Wales by the NCC in its Ancient Woodland Inventory. There are still a few gaps in the coverage, but the extent of decline in most parts of England and Wales is quite clear.

The development of agriculture has also had fairly dramatic implications for the countryside. In 1974 the Countryside Commission (CC) looked at landscape change in seven sample areas in seven counties in lowland England, and found significant changes due to the removal of hedges, ponds and small woods and the shift from mixed farms to intensive arable production. The survey was repeated in 1983, and the trends were shown to have continued, although in the most affected counties studied (Cambridgeshire and Huntingdonshire) they had inevitably slowed since few semi-natural features had survived through the 1970s. Further North and West, in counties like Somerset and Warwickshire, agricultural intensification had taken place later, and with Dutch elm disease had wrought considerable changes between the two studies. In all areas, field sizes had increased (to an *average* of 21.5 ha in Huntingdonshire) and the number of hedges and trees had fallen. Agricultural intensification had created a new, more functional, and less varied landscape. In terms of wildlife, the losses were more serious.

One of the most obvious direct effects of agricultural intensification is the impact of agricultural pesticides. The dramatic effects of the organochlorine pesticides on populations of birds of prey in the 1960s was an important factor in getting them banned from most (but not all) uses more than a decade ago, but many problems persist with the suites of different chemicals applied to arable fields today. Some of the most telling recent research has come from the Game Conservancy's Cereals and Gamebirds Project. For some time it had been known that the grey partridge had declined because of the use of insecticides which killed the

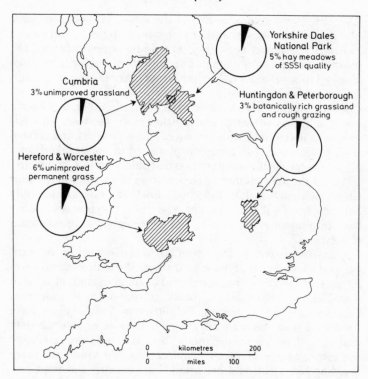

Figure 1.9 The results of studies showing the proportion of grassland in different parts of Britain which remains unimproved.

potential food of young birds. Early in 1985 they announced that some fungicides in widespread use on cereals were also strongly insecticidal. These worked unspecifically, killing many useful species which prey on pests, as well as butterflies and other harmless insects. Without good insect populations, partridge chick survival is very poor, and that means no shooting for the farmer, hence the Game Conservancy's concern. Studies seem to show that even a narrow strip around a field left unsprayed can have dramatic effects on butterfly numbers (particularly brimstone, green-veined white, meadow and hedge brown and small tortoiseshell), and by the same token the number of gamebirds.

35

This may point a way for the future, where farmers care more about their shooting than the last ounce of profit, but it also indicates the impact nationally on wildlife of pesticide use. The effect on conspicuous animals like butterflies and birds has been assessed to some extent. The impact on other taxonomic groups is more or less unknown.

Developments in agriculture have meant that there has been a continuing loss of permanent pasture since the war. This has either been reseeded with improved grass varieties and treated with pesticides and fertiliser, or ploughed up for arable. Figure 1.9 shows the results of surveys carried out by the NCC in the early 1980s of the area of unimproved pasture remaining. In the four study areas across England (both lowland and upland) only between 3 and 6% survives. The other 94% is in intensive rather than traditional management, and is of negligible conservation interest.

Grasslands have, in fact, been particularly hard-hit by agricultural development. Figure 1.10 shows the scale of conversion in just two kinds, grazing marsh and chalk grassland, in selected areas. In Dorset the area of chalk grassland has shrunk from 7700 ha in 1934 to less than 2300 ha in 1972. Losses have continued since then, to the extent that more or less the only chalk grassland left in the country now is in a nature reserve of one sort or another. Grazing marsh can support a number of rare breeding birds (ruff and black-tailed godwit breed in the Cambridgeshire Washes, for example) and also some of the plants of the old undrained fenland. These areas have also suffered considerable losses to agricultural improvement.

Work by John Sheail and Owen Mountford of the ITE highlights the impact of agricultural change on grassland in one area, Romney Marsh in Kent. The area of tillage rose from 9% of the marsh in 1939 to 37% in 1944 in response to wartime policy, but then continued to rise once the war had ended. Large areas were never returned to grassland. By 1950 48% of the farmland on Romney Marsh was under crops, and with the rise in land prices and in investment interest in land in the 1970s, the arable area was maintained. Extensive areas were also drained on the marsh, especially in the 1970s, and by 1980 63% of the marshland had been affected by postwar drainage schemes.

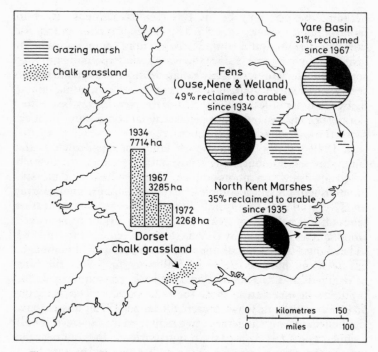

Figure 1.10 The loss of grassland habitats in particular areas of England.

Sheail and Mountford comment 'the impact of the more intensive forms of grassland management, and of cultivation, has now become so extensive as to leave few, if any, refugia for pasture and pasture-dyke species'.

There are still few good studies of land use change and habitat loss in Britain. Data from MAFF come primarily from returns made by farmers, who are generally not particularly aware of areas valuable for conservation, and anyway the survey forms do not have suitable categories to record it. The FC conducted a woodland census in 1984, but as they dismiss most ancient woodlands as 'scrub' because they are of little commercial value, this is a poor source of data for conservationists. Amazingly

37

perhaps, the NCC only began a systematic national survey to monitor habitat change in 1983. This is using air photographs for different periods and a complicated random sampling frame to give data on habitat loss since the war. It will eventually produce some valuable figures, possibly by late 1986 or 1987. By that time several other surveys will have been completed generating similar figures of more or less usefulness, and the picture may be clearer. For the present, we only have piecemeal data on certain counties. None the less, what exists is sobering.

In 1979 the NCC commissioned Ian Langdale-Brown of the University of Edinburgh to study habitat change in lowland Scotland using air photographs. The results (to date still unpublished) present a complex picture of land use change over the 27 years 1946–73. Overall, however, the trend of the loss of semi-natural habitats is clear. The average loss of broadleaved woodland was reported by David Goode in *New Scientist* in 1981 to be about 20%. Average losses of heathland were about 60%, but were as high as 90% in Galloway and 96% in Fife. Marshlands and fens had declined by 10%, grasslands by 35%.

Studies in other areas show the same pattern. *The changing face of Devon* reports work carried out in 1979 by the County Council and the NCC together using maps and field surveys. It tells a similar tale. Only 35% of the rough grazing in the county at the turn of the century remains. NCC studies in Berkshire in 1982 showed declines over only 15 years (1961–76) of 18% in heathlands, 12% in chalk grasslands and 11% in wetlands. There are other studies, more statistics. They all tell the same story, and when the national surveys are completed they will say the same. Throughout the country the area of semi-natural habitat of all kinds has been reduced in extent over the past 40 years faster than ever before. The largest (although by no means the only) culprit has been intensive agriculture.

The fundamental problem is that the supply of rich habitat is far from inexhaustible. There have been gains, of course. Gravel pits can make excellent bird sanctuaries, ironstone mining can create new areas of limestone grassland, and there is a whole new world of urban conservation and habitat creation. However, these created habitats do not even begin to replace those lost, either in terms of extent or the richness of species they support.

Once an area of semi-natural habitat has been destroyed it can never be fully recreated because many of the former species will be unable to re-establish themselves. The more fragmented such areas become, the harder reinstatement will be. For all their skills in environmental management, ecologists can do no more than create an artificial imitation of what has gone.

The amount of land in Britain which is of real interest for its wildlife is now very small in many areas. The NCC surveyed Dorset and Somerset in 1982 to locate all the significant areas of semi-natural habitat which survived. The results are shown in Figure 1.11. Semi-natural habitat accounted for only 13.7% of Dorset and 12.4% of Somerset. In some districts of Somerset the proportion of semi-natural habitat was even smaller (Figure 1.12). Hedges were excluded from both studies, but were estimated to increase the area of semi-natural habitats to 15.5% in Dorset and 14.1% in Somerset. None the less, these surveys suggest that over extensive areas of Britain, and especially in lowland England, there is very little left of great value for wildlife. The countryside may still *look* green, but the area of semi-natural habitat is now very restricted.

However, the loss of wildlife habitat in Britain has not in the past led those who care about it to despair. For over 100 years,

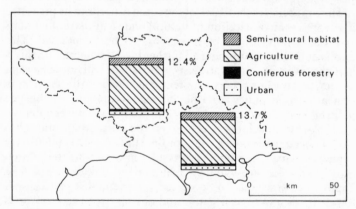

Figure 1.11 The proportion of the area of Dorset and Somerset which comprises semi-natural habitat.

39

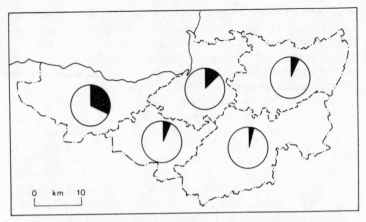

Figure 1.12 The variation in the proportion of each District in Somerset which is semi-natural habitat.

conservationists have been standing up to destructive changes in the countryside, and pushing for new policies from the government. Their main strategy has been to try to protect particularly valuable areas of land in nature reserves, or sites of some other sort. It is this approach which this book is primarily about.

The NCC believes that 10% of the country needs to be protected if a representative selection of natural and semi-natural habitats and viable populations of species are to be maintained. This means quite simply stopping all further loss of habitat, and this is now the target of conservationists in Britain. It will not be easy, as an NCC analysis of the SSSI system concluded: 'Adherence to a firm protection policy does not fit readily into the established political system, which expects compromise wherever interests clash. As far as wildlife is concerned the great compromise has already been made – over 70% of the land surface is intensively exploited. Further compromise results in a gain to the "developer" and a loss to wildlife – real gains to wildlife are almost impossible. Resistance to "progress" in a capitalist society is all too easily dismissed as negative and obstructive. The problem is exacerbated by the fact that natural processes operate within a timescale beyond the scope of even the most assiduous and far-sighted planner; all too often irreplaceable assets are destroyed for short-term financial advantage.' This is a sobering message, because it is obviously one which is far from welcome to the government in the 1980s. It remains to be seen whether it can be put across, by the conservation movement.

Further reading

Body, R. 1982. *Agriculture: the triumph and the shame*. London: Temple Smith.

Body, R. 1984. *Farming in the clouds*. London: Temple Smith.

Bowers, J. K. 1985. British agricultural policy since the Second World War. *Agric. Hist. Rev.* 33(1), 66–76.

Bowers, J. K. and P. Cheshire 1983. *Agriculture, the countryside and land use*. London: Methuen.

Goode, D. 1980. The threat to wildlife habitats. *New Scientist* 22 (Feb), 219–23.

Heath, J., E. Pollard and J. A. Thomas 1984. *Atlas of the butterflies of Britain and Ireland*. London: Viking.

James, N. D. G. 1981. *A history of English forestry*. Oxford: Basil Blackwell.

Mingay, G. E. 1976. *The gentry: the rise and fall of a ruling class*. London: Longman.

Mingay, G. E. (ed.) 1981. *The Victorian countryside*, 2 vols. London: Routlege & Kegan Paul.

Nature Conservancy Council 1984. *Nature conservation in Great Britain*. London: Nature Conservancy Council.

Newby, H. 1980. *Green and pleasant land*. London: Penguin.

Orwin, C. S. and E. H. Whetham 1971. *History of British agriculture 1846–1914*. Newton Abbott: David & Charles.

Parton, A. G. 1985. Parliamentary enclosures in nineteenth century Surrey: Some perspectives on the evaluation of land potential. *Agric. Hist. Rev.* 33(1), 51–8.

Prebble, J. 1969. *The clearances*. London: Penguin.

Ratcliffe, D. A. 1984. Post-medieval and recent changes in British vegetation: the culmination of human influence. *New Phytologist* 98, 73–100.

Ryle, G. 1967. *Forest service*. Newton Abbott: David & Charles.

Sheail, J. and J. O. Mountford 1984. Changes in the perception and impact of agricultural land-improvement: the post-war trend in Romney Marsh. *J. R. Agric. Soc. Eng.* **145**, 43–56.

Shoard, M. 1980. *Theft of the countryside.* London: Temple Smith.

Turner, M. 1980. *English parliamentary enclosure: its historical geography and economic history.* Folkestone: Dawson.

Whetham, E. H. 1978. *The agrarian history of England and Wales. Volume VIII, 1914–1939.* Cambridge: Cambridge University Press.

Williams, M. 1972. The enclosure and reclamation of waste land in Somerset 1700–1900. *Trans. Inst. Br. Geogs* **57**, 99–124.

Chapter Two

Public interest in a private countryside

The preservation of place

Nature conservation in Britain can be said to have begun in the 19th century. It developed out of a widely based and fundamental revolution in the way people thought about nature and what we would now call the environment. This was itself closely related to the increasingly urban nature of society, and its divorce from the countryside. Keith Thomas, in his book *Man and the natural world*, comments that by the 18th century 'a combination of literary fashion and social facts had created a genuine tension between the relentless progress of urbanisation and the rural longing to which an increasing number of people were subject'. This process continued in the next century, and as the countryside was transformed by agricultural improvement, and as the urban population of Britain grew, attitudes to nature changed. A taste for the regular, ordered and productive in landscape gave way to informality and naturalness. Change in society and in the face of Britain in the 19th century fostered a confused yet extremely dynamic view of nature. This was increasingly urban in source and character. Views of the countryside and rural life became increasingly idealised in literature and art. From this odd basis the conservation movement developed.

One forerunner was the remarkable rise of interest in natural history collecting in the 18th and 19th centuries described by

David Allen in his book *The naturalist in Britain*. The collection
of birds, butterflies or flowers became an increasingly popular
amateur pursuit of the leisured classes. By 1873 there were 169
local scientific societies, 104 of them field clubs, with a total
membership of over 100 000. Of course, overcollecting brought
the decline or even extinction of a number of species, but these
very depredations may have stimulated concern for the survival
of rarities. Collectors were also among the first to see the dangers
of the loss of wildlife habitats. The links between nature conservation and natural history have always been strong, and rare
species have always been something of an obsession in both fields.

The 19th century also saw opposition to the persecution of
wild birds. In 1865 a leader in *The Times* criticised the slaughter
of seabirds by 'gentlemen' at Flamborough Head, and four years
later the RSPCA (founded as the Society for the Prevention of
Cruelty to Animals in 1824) supported the Sea Birds Protection
Act 1869. This was followed by others in 1872 and 1880 which
extended protection. A few years later the use of birds' feathers
for hat-making became the target of a series of Victorian
pressure-groups run by women, the Plumage League (founded
1885) and the Fur Fin and Feather League (1889). In 1891 several
groups combined to form the Society for the Protection of Birds,
which became the Royal Society for the Protection of Birds (RSPB)
in 1904. For many years they concentrated their work on the
promotion of effective bird protection legislation.

There was a strongly urban element both to the concern about
the persecution of birds and the interest in natural history. The
protection of particular places, as part of conservation, was an
equally urban initiative, starting at the tail end of the period of
enclosures.

There may have been quite widespread opposition to the
enclosure of open fields in a number of places. In Northamptonshire, for example, local or parliamentary petitions were drawn
up against enclosure in 12% of all parishes enclosed between
1760 and 1800, mostly by small owners and cottagers, and illegal
forms of opposition occurred in a number of cases.

The enclosure of common land frequently provoked opposition. Thus, the enclosure and reclamation of the fen at Otmoor
near Oxford was the focus of protracted opposition from 1786 to

the 1830s: in 1830 prisoners taken by soldiers on Otmoor were released during a riot at St Giles' Fair in Oxford City, and in 1832 special police were recruited to force through the development. The irony here, of course, is that the flat and rich grazing landscape which resulted, where some of the fen plants lingered in the deeper ditches and wetter meadows, was threatened again in 1984 with further drainage to allow cereal cultivation, as another generation of farmers saw the chance to 'improve' it further. Otmoor was also on one proposed route of the M40 motorway (not the one eventually selected late in 1985), and Friends of the Earth (FOE) sold a field in one pound lots to disrupt any attempt at compulsory purchase. In its way their objection to certain kinds of development on private land was essentially the same as that of the early commoners. If early protests about land development smack of FOE and Greenpeace, it is hardly surprising.

There was also opposition to the encroachment of cities and towns onto fields and commons and the enclosure of town fields. There were riots in Leicester in 1754, Warkworth, Burton on Trent, Redditch and Malvern in the 1770s and later at Sheffield, Colchester, Coventry and Oxford, among many other towns. The situation was not always clear-cut. W. G. Hoskins, the landscape historian, contrasts the evil slum development which followed the refusal of the burgesses of Nottingham to allow the town fields to be enclosed with the salubrious sprawl of Leicester whose fields were enclosed, but he points out that at least Nottingham's slum-dwellers could walk in open fields. In Stamford in Northamptonshire the Cecils at Burleigh House resolutely prevented enclosure right up to 1872, and also kept industry out of the town, largely to preserve their control over the election of the Member of Parliament. Stamford fossilised and shrank, while nearby Peterborough on the new railway boomed. It is not clear how this was viewed at the time, but as Hoskins remarks in *The making of the English landscape* 'there are too many Peterboroughs, and not enough Stamfords, in modern England'.

The recreational value of town fields and commons was sometimes recognised quite early, although the response was not necessarily all that a present-day urban conservation manual might recommend. In 1835 the residents of Clapham, south-west of London, acquired the lease to all manorial rights on Clapham Common. They drained it, and made it a public park. It remains a green, if somewhat sterile patch in London's sprawl. Developments were rarely so harmonious. In 1864 Lord Spencer tried to enclose Wimbledon and Putney Commons in Surrey. Local residents opposed the Bill, and he had to content himself with developing a brickpit and a sewage farm. In Stockwell Green (also Surrey), marshy land enclosed 60 years before was built on in 1874 despite attempts to preserve it as open space.

In 1865 the Commons, Open Spaces and Footpaths Preservation Society was formed and co-ordinated opposition to the enclosure of town commons. They fought successfully against the enclosure of Hampstead Heath and Epping Forest, and undertook a notable piece of 'direct action' when a trainload of labourers threw down the fence round Berkhamsted Common overnight. In 1866 and 1869 two Metropolitan Commons Acts were passed preventing the further enclosure of common land within the Metropolitan Police District. In 1871 Wimbledon and Putney Commons were finally preserved by Act of Parliament for public use under the care of conservators. This work was the first on any scale which involved the protection of particular places against development. From it grew the idea of conserving nature by protecting particular areas and habitats in nature reserves or on private land. This has subsequently become the dominant feature of British conservation. Developments began with the work of the National Trust at the start of the 20th century.

A place for nature

The Open Spaces Society could not hold land, and this limited its work. The importance of an organisation which could do so was recognised early in the 1880s, and in 1894 the National Trust for Places of Historic Interest or Natural Beauty was formed. By 1906 it held 24 properties, and the next year the National Trust Act 1907 made the extraordinary provision that the land it held should be inalienable except by decision of Parliament. In 1971 its historian wrote 'the Trust is built on the solid rock of an idea: that the only certain way to protect a building or a piece of land is to own it forever, subject only to the overriding will of Parliament'. A considerable part of the Trust's early effort went into the acquisition of areas which had value for wildlife.

The Trust's first property was 1.8 ha of cliff at Barmouth in Wales, given to the Trust in 1895, followed by the purchase of the Clergy House in Alfriston in Sussex in 1896 and Bawas Head near Tintagel in Cornwall in 1897. In 1899 the Trust bought nine strips of land at Wicken Fen near Cambridge for £10. The Annual Report said it was 'almost the last remnant of the primaeval fenland of East Anglia, and is of special interest to entomologists and biologists'. A further two strips were given to the Trust by Nathaniel Rothschild, and in 1912 a total of 97 ha was donated. In 1902 the Trust's first public subscription was made, raising £6500 to buy 48 ha of Derwent Water in the Lake District, and in 1912, 445 ha of Blakeney Point in Norfolk was 'purchased by a few anonymous individuals and presented to the Trust on condition that the natural flora and fauna should be preserved'.

The membership of the National Trust grew quite slowly, reaching 500 in 1914, only to fall during the war. It reached 500 again by 1921, and continued to grow, rising to 1200 by the end of 1929. Its subscription income remained less than £1000 until the mid-1920s, but increased thereafter, reaching over £4000 in 1935. The number of properties held increased steadily. By 1900 it held ten, by 1910 the number had increased to 40. By 1930 the Trust held 190 properties covering 52 000 ha. Some of these were of importance for their wildlife, for example 84 ha at Hawksmore in Staffordshire acquired in 1926 specifically for its birds, but by no means all. In 1921 the Annual Report mentions some specific natural history interest in only three of the 94 properties listed, which may be an indication of the importance given to it by this stage. Certainly in 1926 the Trust refused to acquire Cley Marshes in Norfolk (where it already held Blakeney Point and Scolt Head), because it was only of interest to naturalists. The Norfolk Naturalists' Trust was therefore established specifically to acquire Cley. It was the first County Naturalists' Trust, and is the oldest by 20 years.

Some felt that the National Trust was too slow to acquire land of high wildlife value at an earlier stage. Nathaniel Rothschild in particular was concerned that the Trust should be encouraged to acquire areas specifically as nature reserves. He was a remarkable man, an able naturalist of the old school, with a vast network of friends and detailed knowledge of places where rare species, especially butterflies, were to be found. He was also wealthy. In 1910 he bought Woodwalton Fen in Huntingdonshire. This was home to a number of rare species, and threatened by over-collecting. It was close to the last home of the Large Copper butterfly, and the site of subsequent attempts at re-introduction in 1927, and again by the Nature Conservancy, in 1968. Rothschild and his friends had an acute sense of the pressures such areas were under from urbanisation, industry and agricultural change. In 1912 they founded the Society for the Promotion of Nature Reserves (SPNR).

Ray Lankester introduced the SPNR in a letter to *Nature* in 1914 'It is proposed to secure, by purchase or gift, the right to preserve from destruction in this country as much and as many as possible of the invaluable surviving haunts of nature'. The value of determined action to acquire specific pieces of land was beyond doubt: 'it is not too late to rescue here and there larger and smaller areas from this awful and ceaselessly spreading devastation'. The National Trust had 'proved itself a capable guardian' of such reserves, and indeed it had already been entrusted with an area of Wicken Fen as well as Blakeney Point. The SPNR hoped it would acquire more. Its aim was 'to collect and collate information as to areas of land in the UK which retain their primitive conditions and contain rare and local species liable to extinction owing to building, drainage, disafforestation, or in consequence of the cupidity of collectors'. All the threats to wildlife are there: urbanisation, agricultural improvement, forest enclosure and clearance, overcollecting.

However, this gives no measure of the intensity of feeling of these early conservationists. Ray Lankester left the scientists reading *Nature* in little doubt about his own position: 'the "country", with its manicured fields, its well-trimmed hedges, and artificial barriers, its parks planted with foreign trees and shrubs, its roadway stinking of tar and petrol, and its streams converted into chemical drains or else over-stocked fish-stews, is only rendered less repulsive than the town by the survival here and there of a pond or a copse or a bit of ancient moor-land (happily too swampy for golfers) where nature is still allowed to pursue her own way without the arrogant interference of that prodigiously shameless barbarian, the "civilised" man'.

This is an astounding polemic, with a sharply contemporary ring to it. It reflects a deepening awareness of the environmental costs of the economic developments in Britain in the 19th century. It is important that at this point the response to this division was seen, by the founders of the SPNR at least, to be the acquisition of land for nature reserves.

Work began at once preparing a list of sites of possible nature reserves throughout Britain. This depended mainly on personal contacts between naturalists, but members of the Botanical Exchange Club (which later became the Botanical Society of the British Isles) and plant ecologists such as E. J. Salisbury, Arthur Tansley and F. W. Oliver who were members of the new British Ecological Society (founded 1913) played a part. Oliver's research on saltmarsh vegetation at Blakeney Point was one reason for wanting to preserve that site. The SPNR's survey was accelerated at the outbreak of war in 1914 because of the threat of the ploughing campaign. A list of 251 reserve sites was given to the Board of Agriculture between 1912 and 1916, although there is little evidence that it influenced their policy.

Despite its forward vision and its influential council, the SPNR achieved little which is tangible at this time. It never had many members, and raised little money. After the war the National Trust declined to form a joint committee. Rothschild fell ill in 1918 and the Society entered a period of relative inactivity, from which it only recovered in the very different conditions of the early 1950s. Although there were other essentially local organisations who also tried to establish nature reserves at about the same time, John Sheail comments in his history of nature conservation, *Nature in trust*, that the SPNR's work remained outside the mainstream of conservation. This was still concerned primarily with matters of cruelty to animals, egg collecting and bird catching. The SPNR itself acquired a few nature reserves, notably Woodwalton Fen donated by Rothschild, but had no programme of acquisition, and no resources to do so. Indeed they had to sell a reserve at Ray Island in Essex to finance management at Woodwalton Fen in 1925. Otherwise, reserves were seen at this period to be merely what John Sheail calls 'a stop-gap measure'. The debate about their usefulness is seen clearly in the experience of the Royal Society for the Protection of Birds (RSPB).

The RSPB's income grew slowly, hovering around £1000 per year before World War I, and then rising to surpass £2000 in 1924 and £3000 in 1927. By the end of the 1930s there were 1100 fellows and 900 members, and an ordinary annual income (excepting legacies) of over £4000. At first the RSPB worked entirely as a pressure group lobbying for stronger protection for birds and control of the plumage trade. However, in 1901 it appointed its first 'watcher', a warden to protect Pintail at Loch Leven, and in 1912 it acquired the shooting lease of Brean Down in Somerset. A committee was set up to oversee this work, and by 1914 22 men were employed to guard 10 areas.

In 1911 the suggestion of 'national sanctuaries' was discussed at the RSPB's annual meeting in the context of the national parks established in the USA and Switzerland. The following August the idea of 'a tract of land stretching across the whole of Europe, even across the globe' was suggested at the Zoological Conference in Graz in Switzerland. Nothing was done in Britain, but the idea of national sanctuaries persisted. The 1922 edition of the RSPB's magazine *Bird Notes and News* again cited overseas experience 'the public and national form of bird sanctuaries has come into being in more recent years, impelled in many cases by the reckless destruction of wildlife by settlers in new lands'. The Board of Works had recently established a committee on bird sanctuaries in the Royal Parks, and the RSPB heralded these 'fairies corners' of city sanctuaries. They tartly commented 'national sanctuaries Great Britain has none. Nor does any part of the cost of preserving the nation's representative bird life flow from the national exchequer to that of the RSPB. The beautiful principle of "voluntary subscription" prevails'.

The RSPB's interest persisted, and influenced for example the work of a government committee set up in 1929 to look into the question of national parks (described below). A year later the RSPB itself acquired its first reserve, at Cheney Court in Romney Marsh in Kent, launching a membership appeal to purchase 180 acres of land. *Bird Notes and News* stated the arguments for the reserve clearly: 'When however it is remembered that constant uncertainty attaches to areas dependent on the goodwill of private owners and the inaction of local Councils, it becomes obvious that a Bird Sanctuary, to be fully successful and worthy of its name, must be stabilised. A Nature Reserve where nature is safeguarded and preserved, not for today only but for future generations, should be vested in the Society permanently and unchangeably'.

In fact the Romney Marsh Reserve was subsequently sold when agricultural drainage destroyed its interest, but from this point the RSPB was launched on a course of land acquisition. In 1930 it acquired 8 acres of East Wood at Stalybridge in Cheshire by bequest (along with £5000 for upkeep) and was given 250 acres of marsh at Denge in Kent. However, it was rapidly found that reserves were vulnerable to changes on surrounding land. In 1932 a member of the RSPB's Council paid £9000 for land in the Greatstones Estate in Kent where the Kentish Plover bred, the RSPB paying the last £2000. However, although the local authority passed a byelaw prohibiting the taking of birds' eggs in the area, the site's value was destroyed by adjacent building development. In 1937 it was resold for its purchase price. None the less, by the outbreak of war in 1939 the RSPB owned 1300 acres at Dungeness and 150 acres in Romney Marsh among a number of other properties, and had helped in the purchase of Ramsey Island in Pembrokeshire as a bird sanctuary. They also owned a small plot and leased a larger area at Brean Down, but again had subsequently to give this up when it deteriorated as a result of housing development and recreational pressure.

While the RSPB was moving slowly towards a policy of land acquisition, in other quarters the idea of *national* nature reserves which would be the responsibility of government was gaining currency. This was closely allied to the parallel idea of national parks, areas set aside for the recreation of urban workers and their families. From the salubrious new 'garden suburbs' to be reached using the extending underground network around London, to the Great Western Railway's 'daffodil specials' to Gloucestershire woods, the British countryside was packaged in the first decades of this century as a calm, unchanging and healing world to which to escape from the towns. It was obviously nothing of the sort, rather from the 1880s onwards it was a place of economic decline, unemployment and debt. Compared with the city environment, however, it seemed a paradise indeed. With the spread of the bicycle at the end of the 19th century and later of the car (of which there were three million on the roads by 1930), demand for countryside recreation by town-dwellers increased.

The world's first national parks were being established in the United States and Canada in the 1880s, for example at Yellowstone and Banff, while the Open Spaces Society was starting its work in Britain. These parks were extensive wilderness areas, taken into federal ownership. Britain had no real wilderness, even then, but the example was not wholly lost here. In 1884 James Bryce brought a Bill to Parliament to allow access to moorlands and mountains 'for recreation, scientific and artistic study irrespective of the wishes of the landowner'. Predictably, this was defeated, as were subsequent Bills in 1908, 1926, 1927 and 1931. However, pressure for such access grew, as the celebrated mass trespass on Kinder Scout in the 1930s and the phenomenal growth of the Youth Hostels Association in the 1930s (established 1930, 83 000 members by 1934) demonstrate.

In 1926 the Council for the Preservation of Rural England (CPRE) was formed, representing 22 constituent bodies concerned with the countryside, and with regional branches. Similar organisations followed in Wales in 1927 and Scotland in 1928. In 1929 the CPRE wrote to Ramsey MacDonald of the new Labour government to ask for an investigation of the need for a series of national parks in Britain. The timing was opportune, and a committee was set up under Christopher Addison, then Parliamentary Secretary to the Minister of Agriculture and already a known proponent of planning. Its report was published in 1931, and suggested three functions for a system of parks. First 'to safeguard areas of exceptional national interest against disorderly despoilation and development', second to improve 'the means of access for pedestrians to areas of natural beauty', and third to promote measures 'for the protection of flora and fauna'. Dartmoor, the New Forest, the South Downs, Snowdonia or the Lake District, and either Cornwall or Pembrokeshire were suggested as possible parks. Some but not all of these have of course subsequently been made national parks under legislation finally passed in 1949.

He was also given a list of possible nature reserves by an organisation called the British Correlating Committee, who argued that recreation and wildlife preservation were irreconcilable. Addison himself certainly foresaw conflict and he suggested separate national parks (primarily for recreation) and regional reserves for nature conservation. The two were easily confused: Stirling Maxwell wrote in *Bird Notes and News* in 1929 'to the ordinary man a National Park and a National Nature Reserve imply the same things, while in point of fact they are essentially and vitally different. The one is for man and welcomes man. The other is for Nature and the protection of Nature from the dominance of the human race'. He seemed to have little patience with national parks: 'the National Park idea has been overlaid with so many suggestions for motor roads, funicular railways, winter sports and hotels at high altitudes that the nature reserve with which the movement started is degenerating into a tea garden'.

Of the two, it was national parks and the recreational function which at that time carried the most political weight. However, although the Addison report was accepted in 1931, the election of a government committed to reducing expenditure temporarily killed off any idea of government involvement in either parks or reserves. Undaunted, the CPRE established a Standing Committee on National Parks in 1934, and maintained pressure. By 1937 the government had started to consider the idea of helping voluntary organisations to protect buildings and scenery, but before that or any other idea could be implemented, war had begun. The depressed countryside once again became the 'home front' and more radical ideas of postwar reconstruction planning came into play. The only parks established at this time were by the Forestry Commission in Argyllshire (1936), the Forest of Dean (1939) and Snowdonia (1940).

National parks and nature reserves

During the war, pressure was maintained on government to take action on both national parks and nature reserves. These ideas became part of planning for the reconstruction of Britain after the war, and were taken on board by the committee headed by Lord Justice Scott on Land Use in Rural Areas in its report in 1942. He proposed nature reserves 'where the prohibition of access shall be the first consideration', and larger national parks. In 1941 the SPNR organised a Conference on Nature Preservation in Postwar Reconstruction, partly at the instigation of the RSPB, at which 19 voluntary bodies were represented. In 1942 this in turn set up a Nature Reserves Investigations Committee (NRIC) to advise on 'reserves, sanctuaries and sites', and to identify endangered animal and plant species.

The NRIC's reports reveal wide-ranging discussion of the functions reserves should serve. G. Dent suggested five types of reserve in 1943, ecological reserves (for research), conservation reserves (for rare species), education reserves, amenity reserves and economic reserves (to encourage the breeding of species beneficial to agriculture). Another contribution defined three aims of nature conservation more generally, a duty of posterity not to lose species or characteristic communities, the promotion of scientific study and education, and the encouragement of appreciation of nature by the general public. He said 'owing to the development of agriculture and industry and the spread of towns, these three objects cannot be secured except through nature reserves'.

In 1943 the NRIC was sent a list of possible reserves by the British Ecological Society. Ecology had developed a long way since Arthur Tansley's involvement with the SPNR's original list in 1916. He had published *The British Isles and their vegetation* in 1939, and this list was an attempt to represent the range of vegetation communities in Britain for the benefit of ecologists. The NRIC itself drew up two consolidated lists of nature reserves and geological reserves in England and Wales in 1945.

Continuing government interest in nature reserves and national parks is shown by the report on national parks by John Dower to the Minister of Works and Planning, published in 1945. This endorsed the notion firmly, and made suggestions of specific areas, while also confirming a need for nature conservation as part of overall government policy. This Report was put to the Reconstruction Committee of the War Cabinet, whose unexciting response was to set up another committee to report on the Report, the Hobhouse committee. In addition, two Wildlife Conservation Special Committees were formed, one for England and Wales and one for Scotland, to advise specifically on nature conservation. The list of members of the committee for England and Wales reads like a who's who of the conservation world, before and since: it was chaired by Julian Huxley; Tansley, Cyril Diver, the animal ecologist Charles Elton, E. B. Ford of the first *New Naturalist* book (on butterflies), Max Nicholson (for 20 years director general of the NC) and the geographer Alfred Steers were all on it, and Richard Fitter was secretary for the first year.

Their report, produced in 1947 (the Scottish committee reported two years later), has become a classic. Its treatment of the reasons for conservation, and its analysis of ways and means, are probably still the most lucid and straightforward statement of what conservation is about even though (or perhaps because) it was not in Civil Service prose. Certainly those principles, and the list of proposed reserves included in the report, were used for many years to come. The report argued the case for government involvement in nature conservation over and above the provision of national parks. 'The further question we have to consider is whether the conservation and study of the flora and fauna is essential to the efficient discharge of the responsibilities of government. To this question we return an unequivocal affirmative'. Reserves and other protected areas were required both within parks and outside in their own right: 'the setting aside of carefully selected parts of the parks which could be more strictly protected from human disturbance and might act as breeding reserves for the particular groups or communities of species it is desired to encourage'. Indeed the committee argued that the idea of 'wildlife sanctuaries' appeared to 'antedate by a considerable period the modern idea of a National Park'.

Above all, the Huxley committee called for a biological service to manage the proposed nature reserves, to carry out research both inside and outside them, and advise the government. Scientific management was vital: 'places of outstanding charm and interest have been "protected" but, through lack of knowledge, indifferent management, or stupidity, their value has waned'. This was a master-stroke. Such was the high esteem in which science in general was held at the end of the war, whose course inventions like radar seemed to have influenced so deeply, that the idea that a biological service and national nature reserves were needed for *science* had enormous appeal. It appears to have taken root in a way that the national parks idea did not. Furthermore the scientific label to an extent hid the extent of the powers proposed for nature conservation. The Huxley committee was at pains to show that the necessary scientific skills could not be developed within the proposed National Parks Commission. In the legislation that followed, the National Parks and Access to the Countryside Act 1949, the provision for nature conservation was far stronger than that for the conservation of landscape or amenity. This fact went virtually unremarked in the Parliamentary debates, and the powers were not trimmed.

The central theme of the Huxley committee's arguments was that of the importance of science, but its main focus was on the loss of habitats, the rate at which 'sites of classical importance in the history of knowledge' were 'disappearing or deteriorating'. It was depressing, they said, to examine the list drawn up by Rothschild in 1915 in the light of the condition of the same sites only 30 years later. 'Some have been irreparably destroyed, others are well on the way to destruction, and more have so declined that they can no longer be rated as of outstanding national importance. The process is still continuing. Nothing would be gained by attempting to apportion blame; but it would be unfair to infer that these sites had mainly been swamped by the advancing tide of bricks and mortar. Many could certainly have been saved, easily and without detriment to schemes for development, had there been an active, informed and centrally directed conservation policy; others are the inevitable casualties of two world wars. They have been lost to hurried and sometimes ill-considered plans for agricultural expansion; to pressing demands for timber; to increasing drainage of surface waters, coupled, but not co-ordinated, with a steadily increasing drain on underground water supplies; and the vital necessity of providing areas for military training, airfields, and defence ... The need to save for posterity the most valuable and interesting of the sites which remain can hardly be denied.'

In response to this picture of the loss of valuable areas, the Huxley committee proposed a sixfold classification of protected land. Their list included National Parks, Local Nature Reserves and Local Educational Reserves, extensive Conservation Areas (discussed in the next section), Geological Monuments and National Nature Reserves. The most central to their purpose were the National Nature Reserves (NNRs), which would each serve one or more of five functions: conservation and maintenance of species, survey and research, experiment, education and amenity. A total of 73 NNRs were listed and described in their report, 85% of them in England and almost all previously listed by the NRIC. It was, they stressed, a list pared to the bare minimum necessary as a basis for scientific research. It was also a list based on scientific principles: 'our selection has been directed to secure a balanced representation of the different major types of plant and animal communities existing in England and Wales, while at the same time including certain unique sites of the highest value to science'.

The total area of the proposed NNRs was less than 70 000 acres, and the value of the land low, because 'the land most suitable for reservation on biological grounds and still available is mainly land which has suffered the least disturbance by man; that is, waste land which has up to the present been, for one reason or another, beyond the margins of economic development, or woodland which is not being exploited commercially to any appreciable extent'. On the same argument, the committee believed the NNRs themselves would conflict little with the interests of forestry or agriculture. They suggested hopefully that the ecological knowledge of the biological service would help the work of the FC and the Ministry of Agriculture.

The Scottish committee developed their argument for conservation on the basis of its potentially great practical economic contribution in their report of 1949. Their job had been much harder, since the NRIC had done no work in Scotland, and they had to appeal widely for information. Their report stressed the 'scientific and economic advantages' of nature conservation, pointing out how the comparison of 'natural balance' with the effects of man would aid the development of agriculture, forestry and fishing. They recommended 50 NNRs, and various other categories of protected land, and called for a separate Scottish Wildlife Service for the conservation and development of natural resources. With this report, the idea of government responsibility for biological research and nature reserves was firmly established in all three countries.

The proposals of the two Wildlife Conservation Special Committees were substantially accepted by the government in 1948, and a single national body, the Nature Conservancy (NC), was created by Royal Charter in 1949. It was given powers under the National Parks and Access to the Countryside Act 1949. These enabled it to acquire land by purchase (compulsory if necessary), or to lease it or conclude a management agreement with the owner, and to declare it and manage it as a NNR. These NNRs were to have a dual role, allowing for scientific research and for the preservation of features of special interest (geological and physiographical as well as biological).

There was some clever footwork by the ecologists promoting the nature conservation cause in the years leading up to the creation of the Nature Conservancy. The ideas of national parks and nature reserves had been linked for so long that the divorce effected by the Huxley committee was opposed by some whose main commitment was to national parks. They believed that the biological service would not be accepted by Parliament, and might jeopardise the whole package of protection. In the event they were proved wrong. The NC was created very much as the Huxley committee had envisaged, while the National Parks Commission lost its proposed planning powers over the same period 1947–49. The 1947 Town and Country Planning Act put planning in the hands of County Councils, and once having gained it they would not yield it again.

John Sheail sums up the story: 'Whereas the provision of parks and greater public access to the countryside aroused keen debate, comparatively little attention was given to nature reserves. The reserves affected fewer people, a much smaller area of land, and were generally cheaper to establish. The concept of National Nature Reserves fitted more easily into the planning framework envisaged by the Town and Country Planning Act of 1947. There would be no conflict with the powers awarded to the county councils in the planning field.' Thus began what Ann and Malcolm MacEwen call 'the great divide' between 'scientific' nature conservation and the conservation of landscape and amenity. This divide persists to the present day, and although a number of NNRs have been established since 1949 by the NC, some of the fundamental problems of conservation have not been resolved. This is most obvious in attempts to conserve areas outside the NNRs, in the ordinary countryside.

Control of land

The movement towards the establishment of nature reserves in the 1920s and 1930s lay wholly within the conventional view of landholding. Indeed the SPNR and to an extent the RSPB had close links with the large landowners. The protection of particular places by acquisition, however, was not the only response to change in the countryside and on the urban fringe. Another approach involved the control of land use change on private land, and this developed as part of town planning. However, it was not initially a strong element in town planning legislation, whose roots lay in a response to the appalling conditions in the 19th century city; a series of reports had sensitised government to the poor health, living conditions and overcrowding of the urban working class at the end of the 19th century.

The first planning Act, the Housing, Town Planning Etc. Act 1909 allowed for (but did not make compulsory) planning schemes drawn up by local authorities or private individuals for land in the course of development or likely to be developed. Like its successors, the Act focused on the town and not the countryside. Its aim was primarily to co-ordinate and promote house construction, but a variety of aspects of new building could be controlled, most notably spacing and density. It introduced into legislation the idea of extending municipal powers over the interests of private developers.

However, planning schemes were not mandatory, and few were made. By 1919 only 13 had been submitted, five of them in Birmingham. One problem was the need to compensate landowners for any loss of value resulting from a planning scheme. In theory any landowner gaining from a plan would have to pay a betterment levy (cut from 100% to 50% during debate of the Bill in the House of Lords), but in practice this was not enforceable.

Authorities feared that by making a scheme they were signing a blank cheque. This problem, which persisted right up to World War II, meant that the only real planning done by most authorities involved those actions exempted from liability for compensation. They could acquire critical areas of land, try to persuade landowners to forego compensation in return for not having their land assessed at building value for death duties, or simply control development by restricting the density of houses allowed. Large areas of the Home Counties were protected in the 1920s and 1930s only by stipulations that houses should be at less than one house per 10 or 25 acres. Low-density development in the countryside went on apace.

In 1919, a second planning Act was passed, intended to help create a 'land fit for heroes'. Once again, the driving force was the need for housing, and the new Act made the preparation of plans compulsory for towns of over 20 000 population. This Act heralded (for better or worse) the interwar housing estate, and saw great official enthusiasm for new residential development in the countryside. One Liberal speaker at the Bill's second reading said 'let us have belts of new housing schemes around our towns, planned and laid out on lines that are spacious and generous in their conception and execution'. Welwyn Garden City was begun the next year, and while the problems of compensation and betterment meant that few town planning schemes were made, a period of rapid urban expansion began. In the two decades between the wars, 4 million new houses were built, many of them in a more or less haphazard manner where developers chose. There were several notable developments on the coast in the south-east, for example Peacehaven in Sussex, where the South Downs met the sea.

This expansion, accelerated by new bus services, growing car ownership and the electrification of London's suburban railways, probably did more than anything else to trigger the alarm of conservationists about the countryside. A typical response was the complaint by a correspondent in *Bird Notes and News* that the whole of England was turning into a 'gigantic garden suburb'. In response to this advance of suburbia the CPRE supported a Rural Amenities Bill put to Parliament in 1929 and 1930 by Edward Hilton Young MP. This defined 'rural amenities' and aimed to extend the power to make plans outside the towns and

60

into the open countryside. The Bill had an unopposed Second Reading, but the Minister of Health stepped in with his own Town and Country Planning Bill in 1931. This was lost with the fall of the Labour government, but was reintroduced in 1932 by Hilton Young, now a minister in a new National Government committed to spending restraint.

In debate, the whole idea of planning took a severe drubbing, both because of the infringement on the private market which it involved, and because of opposition to the adverse effects of the new housing developments which had appeared. The Marquess of Hartington, for example, thought local authorities guilty of 'wholesale vandalism'. The Act was passed in 1932, but achieved very little. Compensation remained, in theory betterment was still payable by landowners, but in practice the system was too complex to work. Plans were once again optional. Through the 1930s, local authorities attempted, with greater or lesser success, to make plans to control development in the countryside, yet the sprawl continued. In 1937, a Parliamentary motion called for a revision of legislation, and the Town and Country Planning Advisory Committee produced a report in 1938 which called for 'rural zones' where 'extensive industry' and housing could be controlled. This provision was introduced in a circular, but had little effect before the war broke out and the whole structure of planning changed.

Throughout the interwar period, the reef on which planning foundered was always that of the control of land. To what extent should, or could, the interests of the community restrain those of the individual landowner or developer? World War II changed the way this question was viewed. In 1941, the Uthwatt Committee on Compensation and Betterment was appointed to consider the question. They commented 'For the last hundred years owners of property have been compelled to an increasing extent, without compensation, to comply with certain requirements concerning their property ... the essence of the compensation problem as regards the imposition of restrictions appears to be this – at what point does the public interest become such that a private individual ought to be called on to comply, at his own cost, with a restriction or requirement designed to secure that public interest?'. The Committee concluded that the common law allowed the State to direct a landowner to refrain from using his land for certain specified purposes, but that this might be unfair (they did not perhaps need to add that it would be outrageously unpopular!). They recognised that the problem needed a solution if local postwar planning was to be effective, and discussed the unification of landownership under some central authority, the extension of compulsory purchase powers, and the acquisition of the State of development rights in land.

To some in Parliament, this was communism under a very thin disguise, and the coalition government creaked at the seams as the ideological implications of the ideas were explored in Parliamentary debates. In the end the Town and Country Planning Act 1944 maintained some semblance of consensus, and compensation was still to be payable (at 1939 prices plus 30%). The matter was, however, far from settled. After the Labour victory in the 1945 election, new legislation was put forward. The Town and Country Planning Act passed in 1947 effectively nationalised development rights in land. In normal circumstances, a landowner would not expect compensation if refused permission to develop. It is on this Act that the whole structure of postwar planning has been based, although in fact the specific question of compensation and betterment has remained a politically hot issue, with the 1947 Act's Central Land Board abolished by the Conservatives in 1953 and a whole series of subsequent arrangements.

The long debate about the control of development rights in land has a particular importance for nature conservation because of the idea that specific *conservation* objectives could be met by a similar approach, the designation of areas of private land where development would be restrained by the conservation interest. The approach was tried first as a way of protecting Ancient Monuments, in Acts passed in 1882 and 1913. This included a list or schedule of monuments (initially 68, rising to 344 in 1921 and 3195 in 1932) and made it illegal for a landowner to cause damage without giving three months notice to the Office of Works. A preservation order could then be issued, giving protection for a period of 21 months, and if necessary Parliament could be asked for a confirming order making the protection permanent. In theory, all the scheduled sites could be protected in this way. If the procedure sounds familiar to a conservationist in the 1980s, this is unsurprising, since the provisions of the Wildlife and Countryside Act 1981 for sssis are essentially the same.

However, these measures were seriously flawed, since the Office of Works was liable either to purchase the site on which an order was placed, or to pay compensation for any loss of value. This it was extremely reluctant to do, with the result that the full powers of the Acts were rarely used. A second problem was that until the Ancient Monuments Preservation Act 1931 was passed, there was no power for protecting the area around monuments. Even then, lack of money and lack of political will greatly restricted what could be done. Despite the apparent adequacy of the legislation, the weakness of the controls on privately owned land made the preservation of monuments rather hit and miss. The editor of *Antiquity* argued in 1929 for the acquisition of the more important sites before prices rose, and before they were lost to afforestation, ribbon development and new roads or aerodromes. His response was like that of the RSPB: purchase was the only way to be sure of the preservation of sites.

Despite the poor record of this approach to the protection of ancient monuments by controlling private land instead of acquiring it, the various committees proposing nature reserves in the 1940s took up the same idea. They identified additional areas, usually of considerable extent, where the nature conservation interest was large, yet where it could be maintained by some kind of presumption against harmful development rather than by purchasing or leasing small reserves. The British Ecological Society suggested 32 'Scheduled Areas' in addition to the 49 National Habitat Reserves, while the NRIC wrote 'some species and associations, or sets of conditions, call for the conservation of large areas'. They added 24 'Conservation Areas' covering 39 000 ha to their list of 47 National Reserves. These were areas where forestry and agriculture were of importance, but the NRIC proposed that no 'drastic or destructive changes' should occur without advice from the proposed 'national reserves authority'.

This idea of designated areas which were only partially under the control of conservationists was fully developed by the Huxley Committee in 1947. They wrote that the fulfillment of the purposes of conservation required the selection of suitable sites 'not all of which call for the same treatment or the same degree of control'. They suggested 'a graded series of sites'. At one end would be the NNR, under strict control. At the other end were 'those sites or larger areas where no greater protection is necessary than to ensure that the possible effects of any proposed changes in land use within their boundaries should, before such changes are actually made, be considered in the light of adequate scientific advice on the varied interests likely to be damaged thereby'. This 'looser type of protection' (to use their phrase) was to be applied to the proposed Geological Monuments, but also to 35 extensive 'Scientific Areas' or 'Conservation Areas'. These covered a total of about 3700 square miles.

This category, borrowed directly from the NRIC, dovetailed with the proposals of the National Parks Committee working in parallel with the Huxley Committee. Conservation Areas 'possess a singular beauty and high scientific interest ... the defacement or disappearance of the distinctive character of such a region involved an irreperable loss which it is hard to over-estimate'. These areas were all part of the same system as the NNRs: without 'reasonable expectation' that these areas would survive without radical change 'far more extensive proposals for reservation would have become imperative or many irreplaceable sites would be lost, and the scientific work so badly needed would be curtailed'.

The committee did not seek 'an overriding voice' for conservation in these areas, only that 'it should be recognised as one of the interests which must be taken into account'. They did not want 'the progress of essential development' to be impeded. They believed that this would be achieved if planning authorities could set aside 'nature zones' which were 'not to be developed except under the stress of exceptional needs'. Development not subject to planning control could be dealt with by liaison with the proposed biological service. Conflicts with forestry could be reconciled by a system of prior consultation with the FC, and liaison should avert 'undesirable repercussions on the natural equilibrium' caused by injudicious agricultural development. An independent tribunal should arbitrate conflicts of interests over mineral developments. Land drainage was a bigger threat to conservation, but the right approach was a fundamental scientific and economic survey of water resources, not any specific controls over the drainage of special areas.

The first need was for the biological service to survey the proposed conservation areas (or scientific areas as the Huxley Committee chose to call them), 'at the earliest possible date in order that a schedule may be drawn up setting out the precise features and sites within it which are considered to be of the greatest scientific value'. In *addition* the Huxley Committee proposed that a separate national list of other 'Sites of Special Scientific Importance' should be drawn up. Throughout the country there were 'many hundreds of small sites of considerable biological and other scientific importance, the great majority of which could easily be safeguarded from destruction if their value and interest were but known to their owners and the appropriate authorities'. This schedule should include all sites 'considered to be of sufficient importance to warrant scientific intervention in the event of their being threatened with dangerous interference or obliteration'.

In the event, the Conservation Areas – like many other aspects of the proposed landscape conservation and national parks system – did not reach the statute books in the National Parks and Access to the Countryside Act 1949. Without the Conservation Areas for landscape, the Scientific Areas were also omitted from the legislation. Only sssis were mentioned in the Act. So instead of some measure of protection for conservation sites over extensive tracts of country, the newly created NC was left with a much more limited power. It could only point out the scientific interest of such smaller sites as it scheduled to local authorities.

The Act read 'Where the Nature Conservancy are of the opinion that any area of land, not being land at present being managed as a nature reserve, is of special interest by reason of its flora, fauna or geological and physiographic features, it shall be the duty of the Conservancy to notify this fact to the local planning authority in whose area the land is situated'. As it happens, the pace of countryside change in Britain since 1949 has made this clause one of the most significant of the whole Act. Its limitations are only now being realised.

Further reading

Allen, D. E. 1976. *The naturalist in Britain*. London: Penguin.

Charlesworth, A. (ed.) 1983. *An atlas of rural protest 1548–1900*. London: Croom Helm.

Cherry, G. E. 1975. *Environmental planning. Volume II, National Parks and recreation in the countryside*. London: HMSO.

Cherry, G. E. 1982. *The politics of town planning*. London: Longman.

Gilg, A. W. 1978. *Countryside planning: the first three decades 1945–1976*. London: Methuen.

Hoskins, W. G. 1955. *The making of the English landscape*. Sevenoaks: Hodder and Stoughton (Penguin edition 1970).

Huxley, J. S. 1947. *Conservation of nature in England and Wales*, HMSO cmd 7122. London: HMSO.

Sheail, J. 1974. *Nature in trust: The history of nature conservation in Britain*. London: Blackie.

Sheail J. 1980. *Rural conservation in inter-war Britain*. Oxford: Oxford University Press.

Thomas, K. 1983. *Man and the natural world: changing attitudes in England 1500–1800*. London: Allen Lane (Penguin edition 1984).

Chapter Three

Conserving the countryside

An integrated countryside?

The provisions made for nature conservation in 1949 had one major and vital flaw. There were no planning powers against the development of agriculture and forestry. Planning was channelled into a focus on the specifically urban threats to the countryside of urban sprawl, ribbon development and uncontrolled industrial development. The protection of the countryside from the spreading town had been an important element in town planning from the 1930s onwards. Patrick Abercrombie was a member of the Barlow Committee on the Location of Industry and Industrial Population. In a dissenting minority report he said 'in Victorian times, the introduction of factors inimical to well-being was largely confined to the towns. We however, with our improved means of communication, have despoiled the countryside and largely diminishd the areas in which health-giving elements of the countryside continue to flourish, and this is just at the moment when they have become most consciously valued'. He argued that 'a substantial stretch of the countryside may have its rural characteristics largely destroyed without the emergence of anything which could be described as a town, with town advantages'.

Early commentators on planning concentrated on this paradox in which spread of towns at the expense of the countryside was paralleled by rising concern for conservation. Thomas Sharp, for example, wrote in his book *Town planning* in 1940 'we bemoan the change, make feverish little efforts here and there to save a "beauty spot". And all the while we betray our own littleness, our timidity, our lack of spirit'. He was clear that 'the way to save the countryside from destruction is to make the towns fit to live in'. Countryside conservation was clearly seen to be part of the town planners job, and, equally, the main threats to the countryside were from the town.

The NC's power to schedule SSSIs for local authority planners was conceived of as an appropriate way of meeting that urban threat to the countryside. It was far from trivial, but in the postwar period it was found to be inadequate to meet the scale of change in agriculture, and the continued expansion of forestry. The planners were, to modern eyes, strangely unconcerned by the impact of agriculture on the countryside. Abercrombie wrote in *Town and country planning* in 1983 that with agriculture development a good deal of 'precious history in greenery' would 'have to go', to be replaced by 'sweeps of open, highly-cropped fields'. This was good forecasting, but he believed the new landscapes would have a sufficient beauty of their own. Like many commentators whose interest is primarily the look of the landscape he did not look beyond that to the poverty of the transformed eco-systems in wildlife terms.

This view was common among those planning for the country-side at this period. The apparently self-evident need for agri-culture to be prosperous was accepted, and the extent and speed of the changes both in the wildlife interest of the farmland itself and in semi-natural habitats was not appreciated. This failure of perception was clear in the Report of the Committee on Land Utilisation in Rural Areas set up under Lord Justice Scott in 1940. There were really two reports, one by a majority of the commit-tee, and one by Professor S. R. Dennison, an economist of the University of Wales. The majority were almost platitudinous about agriculture: there was 'no antagonism between use and beauty', the landscape was 'a striking example of the inter-dependence between the satisfaction of man's material wants and the creation of beauty'.

This belief in the essential rightness of agricultural manage-ment and its benevolent effects on the countryside led the committee to two erroneous conclusions. First, they thought that farming was not only the cheapest but also the only way of conserving the 'traditional aspect' of the countryside. Second, because the kind effects of agriculture stemmed from 'an innate love of nature deeply implanted into the heart of man' they believed that at all costs farmers and farm labourers should be kept on the land and the industry be maintained at its current size and in its traditional (largely unmechanised) state. They also suggested that to protect farmland against urban growth, it should be made inalienable except in the case of overriding national need.

The *Economist* castigated this as 'vague romantic flubdub', a view presumably in part shared by Professor Dennison. He saw no reason to favour farming over other industries, and argued that the problem of the loss of agricultural land to urban uses was exaggerated. Agriculture must become more efficient and more mechanised, and the shedding of agricultural labour, far from being a major problem was a major contribution to efficiency. Certainly, the majority report of the Scott Committee was slow to recognise the transformation wrought by the war, particularly in the spread of mechanisation. In 1939 there were only 52 000 tractors in use in England and Wales, by 1943 125 000, with a tenfold increase in the number of combine harvesters over the same period. The Scott Committee was so preoccupied with the prewar agricultural depression that it mis-diagnosed the ailments of the countryside, and its prescription was anodyne. Dennison's hard-bitten alternative view held little of comfort for conservation.

The idea that farmed land had a high conservation value was widespread among conservationists, but not universal. In 1943 a correspondent to *Bird Notes and News* wrote 'no lover of nature can fail to be alarmed as to the effects which the great changes, now taking place in the countryside, must have upon the future welfare of our native wild flowers, insects, birds and beasts'. The changes he had in mind included mechanised farming, hedgerow removal, loss of hedgerow timber, agricultural drainage, the coniferisation of broadleaved woodland and 'the remorseless tidying up of all rough corners'.

Four years later the Huxley Committee examined the potential conflicts between conservation and agriculture. Nature reserves were on poor land. Ploughing this meant that 'Sites of the greatest scientific and cultural value are irrevocably destroyed for the most meagre short-term return in crops. Such a policy is thoroughly unsound'. More serious were the 'drastic changes in the landscape' caused by development in agricultural techniques and machinery, and in particular land drainage. 'Agricultural advance in the last century has been intimately linked with the improvement of surface drainage, with the result that many thousands of acres of marsh and fenland have been converted into first class agricultural land. Not only are these types of vegetation often of the highest scientific interest, but, as the Nature Reserves Investigations Committee points out, they very rapidly disappear and once lost are gone forever'. There were conflicts too with forestry: 'the application of good sivicultural methods may in certain types of wood be antagonistic to research interests or even completely destroy the biological value of a site'.

The legislation of 1947 and 1949 left a gap in the provisions for habitat conservation of enormous proportions. The transformation of the agricultural industry after the war under the influence of government policy of course had a major effect on the countryside. Agricultural and forestry activities were exempted from planning controls, and there was effectively no check on how the vast majority of the countryside was managed. In 1937 A. G. Street, author of *Farmers' glory* warned farmers against 'short-sighted national policy which bribes them to rob their land of its fertility' by increasing their grain production at the expense of stock farming. He wrote 'I cannot think that any townsman wishes to see an English countryside from which the trees and hedgerows have vanished, and in which mechanical monstrosities make the rural scene hideous by day and noisy by night. But unless our townsfolk wake up to the danger quickly, the countryman may be forced by unthinking politicians to despoil our countryside of its fertility and charm in order to pay his way'.

This picture, written just before the war, is as good a description as any of what happened in farming after it. The study group on technology in the countryside at the Second Countryside in 1970 Conference held in 1965 (of which more later) recorded how 'increase in efficiency inevitably leads to intensification, and requires larger farms and removal of many hedges ... with ...

70

more uniformity of crop over a larger area and the substitution of piped water for the traditional pond'. This was a seemingly inevitable progression, in as much as the changes followed each other in a piecemeal way without sudden transformations although it was an inevitability born of deliberate policy not natural law. The NFU representative at the same conference stated the accepted wisdom: 'the prime function of our countryside is to grow food, to grow it well, in abundance and efficiently ... with the help of every mechanical aid which the second great agricultural revolution of the past 20 years has both provided and demanded'.

Indeed the juggernaut of agriculture, with its crowd of devoted worshippers, trundled onwards and the countryside was transformed at an unprecedented rate. The NFU man complained that 'to listen to some of our critics, one would imagine that modern agriculture had reduced East Anglia to a hedgeless prairie, covered Green Belts with acres of broiler houses, invaded the natural beauty of Exmoor with the all-destroying plough, and reared tower silos on every vantage point and beauty spot'. His righteous indignation was ill-founded. 'Modern agriculture' had done all these things, and if it had not yet, it was soon to do so. The nature conservation movement, with its NNRs and SSSIs (as they became known) found itself able to do little or nothing to stop it.

The science of conservation

Despite the shortcomings of the conservation legislation, there was boundless enthusiasm for the task in hand in the young NC in the early 1950s. Initial progress was slow, with only a third of the first year's money being used, but by March 1950 the Conservancy had 26 staff (8 of them scientists) based in Edinburgh and London. Eighteen months later, in November 1951, the first NNR was declared at Beinn Eighe. This was followed by eight other reserves in 1952, including Holme Fen in Huntingtonshire, Yarner Wood in Devon, the famous Yew Wood of Kingley Vale in Sussex and Moor House on the highest point of the Pennines (Fig. 3.1). The NC also had responsibility for geological and

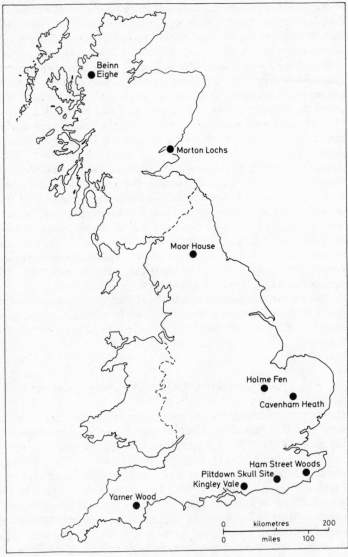

Figure 3.1 The first national nature reserves declared in Britain (declared by 31 May 1952).

physiographic conservation, and the site where the skull of Piltdown Man had been found was also declared an NNR, although this declaration was rapidly revoked when the hoax was unmasked.

Sir Arthur Tansley, the same ecologist whose work was known to Rothschild in 1912, was the first chairman of the NC. The first director-general was Cyril Diver, who was followed by the charismatic and controversial figure of Max Nicholson. However, the early years of the Conservancy were far from plain sailing.

The main thrust of the NC's work was the protection of habitats through the declaration and management of NNR and the scheduling of SSSIs, and a considerable amount was achieved. Also important was the scientific and advisory work, and here there were difficulties. The Huxley committee had wanted a biological service which could moniter and guide developments in all environmental fields. However, in the same way as the entrenched interest of county planners meant that planning powers were not given to the national park authorities, there were interests jealous of the wide remit of the NC.

Research stations were opened at Merlewood in Lancashire in 1953, and at Furzebrook in Dorset in 1954. An experimental station was built on a green field site next to Monks Wood NNR near Huntingdon in 1961. Among other areas of research it became the centre of work on the effects of organochlorine pesticides on wildlife. This is arguably the most outstanding scientific contribution yet to nature conservation in Britain. The story is described in John Sheail's recent book *Pesticides and nature conservation: the British experience* (1985). To simplify, work in Britain and America established links between the use of organochlorine pesticides, like Dieldrin and DDT, and the decline of predators, particularly birds of prey. These chemicals were a major element in agriculture's search for greater efficiency and productivity, and their use was promoted by an increasingly powerful agrochemical industry. However, the evidence was eventually conclusive enough to get these particular pesticides banned for most uses in Britain.

The NC's work had not gone unopposed, however. In 1958 criticism brought investigation from the Select Committee of

Estimates of the House of Commons. This was a setback, but in fact the Committee found little to complain of: modest facilities, real problems being tackled, and a lot of hard work. The NC survived.

However, the concept of a broad and integrated role for conservation did not. By 1949 the interests of other rural land users, particularly forestry and agriculture, were thoroughly entrenched, and brooked no involvement with or adjudication over their activities, regarding both research and advice as an unwarranted intrusion. The NC, and with it conservation as a whole, was pushed into a peripheral position and an increasingly antagonistic stance on rural land use, as much by this administrative opposition as the increasingly destructive practices in the countryside itself. The NC grew, and protected small areas, but the scope of their action was severely constrained. *Nature conservation in Great Britain*, published in 1984, says simply that 'the inability to develop a broader kind of nature conservation should be regarded as the nation's failure: the opportunity was there but it was not taken'.

The NC has gone through several incarnations. Before 1965 it had come under the science minister in government, but in that year its scientific role (but not its growing concern with land acquisition and protection) was stressed by placing it under the newly-created Natural Environment Research Council (NERC), funded through the Department of Education and Science. It was not wholly a change for the better as the NC became absorbed into the larger organisation. The following year Max Nicholson ceased to be director-general, and Barton Worthington, head of the scientific branch, left as well. A period of constrained income and reduced influence followed, with an apparently growing mismatch between increasingly reductionist ecological research, and the executive demands of conservation, particularly site protection. In 1973 the two sides split, the executive part becoming the NCC, under the Department of the Environment (DOE) in the Nature Conservancy Council Act 1973, and the research side remaining in NERC as the ITE.

Thus it has remained, a somewhat uneasy division of old friends. Many a conservationist lurks inside a wholly scientific skin in an ITE becoming more streamlined and contract-oriented by the year, and many in the NCC regret the passing of the old communion between pioneering ecology and active conservation. The idea was that the NCC should commission research from ITE, but as ecology has moved away from the old habitat-based work of Tansley and the early pioneers towards experimentation, the NCC has had to look elsewhere for answers to the many basic questions it faces. Its own chief scientist's team was established (now renamed a directorate) and has evolved into an in-house advisory service as much as a research commissioning agency. However, research money is tight, and there are still important gaps in knowledge of a basic sort about the distribution and status of organisms and communities.

Ironically, it is now ITE which seems more likely to form the nucleus of a research-based biological agency to advise government about resource use, perhaps with parts of the FC and the Agriculture and Food Research Council. The NCC has become a sectional agency, almost a pressure group within government, where once it portrayed itself as more impartial, open to all land use interests and above sectional views of the countryside. Its task now is clear under the terms of the 1973 Act: to advise government about what is best for nature conservation. The NCC's promotional role for conservation is essentially similar to that of the Ministry of Agriculture for farming. In the words of Chris Rose, countryside campaigner for FOE in 1984, 'the reconciliation of land use conflicts is not in its province'.

The NCC has been somewhat reluctant to change, and slow to do so. It has been reluctant to abandon a belief that 'science' was a magic wand which would justify what it wanted to do, and win respect and support from other land users and within government. Apart from the attitudes of other land users, two developments have helped 'radicalise' the NCC, if one may use the word of an organisation still trapped by its own civil service rectitude. The first is the fact that despite its best efforts the loss of semi-natural habitats went on unchecked. The second is the rise of the conservation movement as a whole, and in particular the growth of the non-governmental nature conservation organisations. This has broadened pressure for action on habitat loss far beyond the narrow circle of university scientists and established naturalists who conceived the NC. These changes fostered a far more outspoken stance on habitat and species loss.

The conservation movement

There was an explosion of interest in conservation in its broadest sense and in environmental issues such as pollution, in the 1960s and 1970s. The membership of conservation organisations like the RSPB and the National Trust soared. At the end of the war, the RSPB still had a small membership of 5300, and an ordinary income of less than £6000. The membership topped 10 000 by the end of the 1950s, reaching almost 30 000 in 1965, and 67 000 in 1970. By 1965 it held 25 reserves covering 2800 ha, and had launched an appeal for £100 000. A decade later membership stood at over 200 000 and the reserve holding about 16 000 ha. In that year, they launched the 'Save a Place for Birds' appeal, reaching its target of £1 million. By 1978 they held 31 000 ha of reserves, and both membership and landholding were increasingly steadily. Including the Young Ornithologist's Club, membership is currently near 0.5 million, and the RSPB holds 95 reserves covering 47 600 ha.

This success story is matched by that of the Naturalists' Trust movement. The Norfolk Trust (established 1926) was still unique at the end of the war, but was then joined by Yorkshire (1946), Lincolnshire (1948) and in 1956 by Leicestershire, and Cambridge and the Isle of Ely. Their combined membership was 1300 people. In 1956 the SPNR established a County Naturalists' Trusts Committee. The number of Trusts grew. By 1984 there were 46 Trusts with a total of 150 000 members. Between them the Trusts held some 1500 nature reserves, some of them very small, but in total covering about 55 000 ha. The SPNR changed its name to the Society for the Promotion of Nature Conservation (SPNC), and in 1981 became the Royal Society for Nature Conservation (RSNC).

If success were to be measured by the number of paid-up supporters or the acreage of reserves, the conservation movement has been successful. Measured by other criteria, however, the record is less good. Even as the membership grew, habitat loss continued, seemingly unchecked by the planners, the Conservancy or the voluntary bodies. In May 1963 National Nature Week was organised, and one of the events, the Observer Wild Life Exhibition, showed the extent of the problem and the lack of available solutions. At the instigation of the Duke of Edinburgh, a conference was hastily organised for the autumn, titled grandly *The countryside in 1970*. Much to everyone's surprise this 'bold experiment' was a success, with 200 people from 90 organisations reaching some measure of understanding, if not unanimity.

A second conference, under the same title, was organised two years later. Twelve study groups met through 1965 to prepare papers for the meeting in November. This was a better organised affair, and more hard-hitting. A great many deep-seated concerns about the countryside were aired. Max Nicholson, who reviewed the preparatory studies, wrote 'we are confronted with strangely unfamiliar and disturbing trends, implying drastic and often unwelcome changes in the traditional friendly landscape, the comfortable and settled ways and the pace of movement in the countryside'. Less abstractly, a man from the National Trust said 'For many years now, I have been horrified by the threats to this lovely countryside of ours. I must say that, having read through a high percentage of the reports for this Conference, I really almost give up hope. I had no idea there were so many ghastly things happening'.

Max Nicholson hailed the work of the study groups as 'at last an explicit and articulate basis for arriving at a contemporary and agreed national policy towards the countryside'. It gave 'a taste of the exhilarating and encouraging experience of ceasing to drift and worry and watch things deteriorate'. Indeed, for a while the conference did have a significant impact on provisions for countryside conservation. The study groups called for a much stronger body to oversee not only national parks but also the rest of the countryside. At the conference, the Minister of Land and Natural Resources announced the government's intention to create a new Countryside Commission out of the old National Parks Commission, with new powers.

This was eventually done in the Countryside Act 1968, which also included the provision that Ministers should 'have regard for' conservation in the exercise of their duties (although it also laid a reciprocal duty on the Nature Conservancy to have a regard for agriculture, which largely cancelled out the gain). However, the conference did not question agricultural policy, and did little to alter the attitudes of farmers and foresters themselves. The report of the second conference repeated the accepted wisdom that 'the prosperity of agriculture and forestry are of primary importance in the national economy, in the management and care of the countryside, and in the creation of good landscape'. The NFU representative stressed that agriculture 'must not be confused by restrictions which farmers cannot understand and do not consider necessary'. Despite the establishment of a standing committee to carry forward its work, the conference faded out without making a permanent impact. A third and final conference was organised in 1970 itself, which was also designated European Conservation Year. Nothing significant had changed for habitat protection.

The conferences did not create a co-ordinated conservation movement. In September 1966, the suggestion was to put to the County Naturalists' Trust Conference in Bournemouth that they, the SPNR and the RSPB should all combine in one organisation. Two years of debate followed about this merger, and a further one with the Council for Nature. They never occurred, and the conservation movement remained dislocated in practice and disunited in appearance throughout the 1970s. In their own worlds, work went on intensively to build up membership and expand their reserve holding.

There were also other initiatives, notably perhaps the formation of the Farming and Wildlife Advisory Group (FWAG) following a successful conference on Birds and Farmland at Silsoe in 1969. FWAG has been an exercise in consensus-creation. It has now expanded to have groups in most counties, and full-time advisers, but despite its good work, it is not an organisation intended to influence government policy. It therefore had little effect on habitat loss. For that, conservationists still looked in the 1960s to one of two measures, the nature reserve and the SSSI.

Site protection

In 1962 Norman Moore wrote of nature conservation that it 'consists principally of the selection, acquisition and management of land, and scientific research'. Reserve acquisition began early in the life of the NC. By 1953 11 NNRs had been declared, and more were in the pipeline. The Conservancy felt a responsibility to achieve 'a considerable acceleration of the acquisition and declaration of new NNRs which cannot be retarded unless sites of irreplaceable importance are to be lost'. By the following year, there were 20 NNRs, but 'too many proposed reserves still await detailed survey and the opening of negotiations'.

By 1960 there were 84 reserves, covering a total of 56 250 ha. The Huxley and Ritchie Committees together had limited their list of reserves to a total of 101, covering 73 000 ha. These figures were exceeded by 1963 (105 reserves covering 88 000 ha) and the number continued to climb. By 1985 there were over 190 reserves totalling 150 000 ha, and the 200th NNR was declared late in 1985 (Figs 3.2 & 3).

This expansion over and above the plans of the 1940s was quite deliberate, and primarily a response to the inadequacy of the measures at the Conservancy's command to combat habitat loss. However, the Conservancy's acquisitiveness led to difficulties. There was a lack of data on the new reserves, and of knowledge on how to manage them. As for acquisition plans, the Wildlife Conservation Special Committee lists were revised and expanded, and were to have been published as an appendix to the Annual Report of 1955. This was suppressed because of the sensitivity of admitting to an expanded 'shopping list' quite as openly as this. The problem persisted, however, because as reserve acquisition continued and other sites were destroyed it became necessary to update the list of sites worthy of being NNRs. In 1965 the Conservancy therefore began a new country-wide survey of natural and semi-natural habitats. By 1970 a definitive list of 'key sites' was available. It took a further seven years to be published, during which time further sites were added, and others deleted because of damage. The result, *A nature conservation review*, was published in two volumes by Cambridge University Press in 1977.

In theory, all the sites in 'A Nature Conservation Review' were worthy of being national nature reserves. By 1980 only a fifth were protected. The NCC wrote in its annual report 'although we accept that much of the land concerned can appropriately be conserved in other ways, we need to be able to act when there is a new threat to a key site or an unrepeatable opportunity to

79

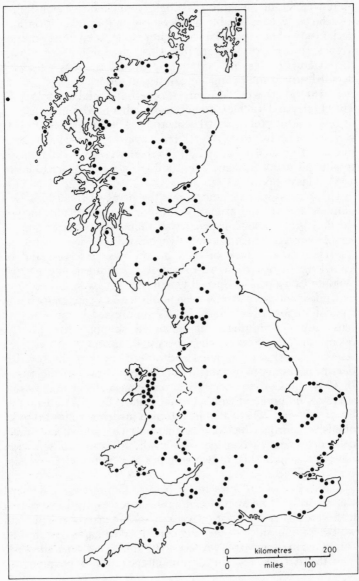

Figure 3.2 The location of national nature reserves in Britain, 1985.

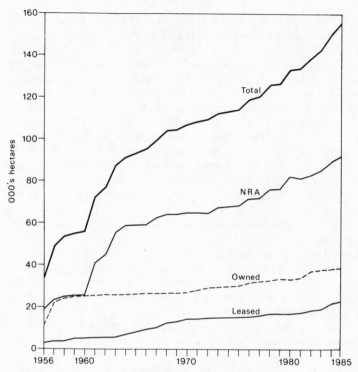

Figure 3.3 Growth in the area of land in national nature reserves in Britain.

safeguard one'. This the NNC has never been able to do, because they have been too tightly constrained in finance. The problem began early. In 1955 Carstairs Kames in Lanarkshire was under consideration as a geological NNR. The local authority wanted to extract sand and gravel from the site, and the NC 'were reluctantly forced to conclude that they could not justify asking for a large sum of public money needed to acquire and sterilise these deposits'. The site was therefore left unprotected, and indeed the view that the NC should not retain an area as an SSSI which they had formally agreed could be exploited out of existence led them to remove the site from the SSSI Schedule.

There has always been a discreet veil drawn over the Conservancy negotiations for land, and as a result it is hard to know how often dilemmas of this sort materialised. They have probably been quite frequent. Certainly, the imperative to expand the number of NNRs at minimum cost led the Conservancy to make extensive use of leases and Nature Reserve Agreements (NRAS) instead of buying land outright. The first reserves held under NRA were declared in 1954, and by 1956 57% of the total area of reserves was held under agreement, and a further 8% was leased. The proportions have increased over time. Of the 150 470 ha in NNRs in March 1985, 60% was held under NRA, 15% was leased, and only 25% (just over 38 000) was owned. Most of the leased or NRA area is in Scotland (68%). Only nine NNRs in Scotland are wholly owned, and in Britain as a whole, 61% of reserves are wholly or partly held under lease or NRA. The protection of these areas depends on the NCC's ability to renew the leases and agreements. This depends primarily on the NCC's funds. A number of leases are starting to run out in the 1980s. Looked at in this light, the NNR series is far from completely secure, and the Conservancy's apparently impressive achievement something of a conjurer's illusion.

Perhaps because of the increasingly obvious discrepancy between the extent of change in the countryside and the best

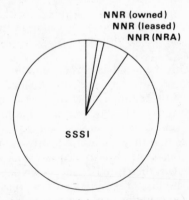

Figure 3.4 Comparison of the area in Britain in sites of special scientific interest and in national nature reserves.

response the NCC could produce in terms of NNR declaration, the importance of SSSIs has grown. In *Nature conservation in Great Britain*, published in 1984, the NCC commented ' the SSSI device gradually proved to be a more effective means of safeguarding important areas than had originally seemed likely'. After the NC's establishment in 1949, work began rapidly on the preparation of county SSSI Schedules which could be considered in the statutory plans which had to be ready by 1952. The basis of these were the lists prepared in the 1940s by the regional committees of the Nature Reserves Investigations Committee. Progress was brisk. By September 1962, 1726 SSSIs had been identified, 73% of them in England, and almost half of them geological sites. Regular revision of the Schedules began. By 1975 there were 3209 SSSIs, and by 1984 over 4000 sites covering 1.3 million ha. Their aggregate extent was 10 times that of NNRs in 1984 (Fig. 3.4). The SSSI system was certainly extensive. Unfortunately it was singularly ineffective.

Planning authorities were notified of the value of SSSIs, and in some (although by no means all) cases they did take this into account. But agriculture and forestry, wholly uncontrolled by the planners, were doing extensive damage. There are few reliable figures, largely because when the SSSI schedules were revised, sites deleted or reduced in area were rarely recorded, and old schedules were not systematically kept. None the less, John Sheail records that, by 1975, 113 sites had been removed from the schedules, presumably because of damage and 87 reduced in area. Together, these 200 sites represented 8% of biological SSSIs scheduled at that time. This is likely to be only part of the damage. An example of the reduction in the size of an SSSI is shown in Fig. 3.5. Work by Barton and Buckley shows how the area of Wye and Crundale Downs SSSI in Kent shrank as the chalk grassland habitat was lost to afforestation or agricultural change. The encroachment of scrub due to reduced rabbit grazing following the outbreak of myxomatosis in the 1950s has also been a problem on this site.

The inadequacy of the SSSI system did not go unnoticed. In June 1964 Marcus Kimball MP introduced a Private Member's Bill to Parliament 'to make provision for the better protection of areas of special scientific interest, and for purposes connected therewith'. It was not given a second reading. The following year,

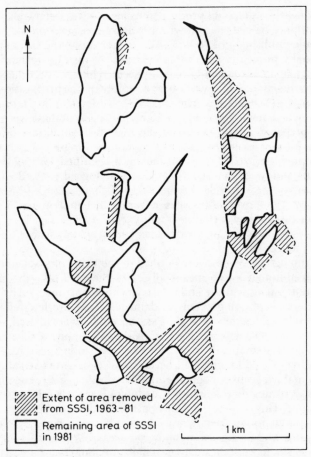

Extent of area removed
from SSSI, 1963–81

Remaining area of SSSI
in 1981

1 km

Figure 3.5 Reduction in the area of Wye and Crundale Downs SSSI
1963–81.

the study group reviewing legislation for the Second Countryside in 1970 Conference recommended the removal of agriculture's exemption from planning controls on all sssis, and the 'removal of any obligation for the Minister of Agriculture to make ploughing grants in respect of an sssi'. Lord Hurcomb, Chairman of the study group, spoke of their unwillingness to see 'further wastage of irreplaceble scientific assets', and called for compensation 'in suitable cases where the owner is asked to refrain from doing something otherwise permissible'. Both recommendations were omitted from the summary report of the Conference.

An attempt by Marcus Kimball to include provision in the 1968 Countryside Act to bring sssis under planning control (on the strength of the study group's recommendations) was unsuccessful. The only proposal of the study group which was implemented was that the Conservancy should be empowered to make agreements and payments to the owners of sssis. Section 15 of the 1968 Act allows for management agreements with the owners of sssis. Small numbers of sites were protected in this way, usually small sums being offered to amenable owners. However, the loss of sssis continued.

The control of countryside change

As agricultural intensification took place through the 1960s the area of the countryside of high wildlife value declined. Following EEC entry in 1972 the pace of development did not slacken, indeed if anything it intensified. In 1975 the government produced a White Paper *Food from our own resources* which set a target of further growth in agricultural production, justified in terms of high food prices and price fluctuations expected within and outside the EEC. It was argued that this 'should not result in any undesirable changes in the environment'. Grazing on hill land could contribute to 'a better-looking as well as to a more productive countryside'. The government claimed that its proposals in the White Paper could be reconciled with 'their commitment to proper safeguards for the environment'.

This was either wishful thinking or ignorance. In 1977 the NCC published its own paper, *Nature conservation and agriculture*, a calm and polite inquiry into the impacts of agricultural change. This stated 'agricultural and other development removes features of the environment on which many species depend. If farmers, foresters and builders of towns and factories do their jobs effectively under current arrangements, these effects are unavoidable, and it is no use blaming them'. Instead, they should be given 'appropriate responsibilities and commensurate resources' to do something for conservation.

The report came up with a series of suggestions, the central pillar of which was a call for a national land use strategy which would specifically give nature conservation a place among national objectives, and recognise that 'wildlife is a vital part of the real capital wealth and heritage of the nation'. In retrospect it is clear that it was an illusion that such a strategy (were it feasible for other reasons) would allow much space for conservation. The whole problem was (and is) that conservation does not make anyone much money. Neither landowners or the state will support it against more profitable enterprises beyond a certain point. *Nature conservation and agriculture* suggested that a national land use strategy would 'foster a rational approach to resources and would provide a framework within which the priorities of different land uses could be related and harmonised'. This was a mirage. Either damaging activities would have to be controlled in the national interest, or conservation had to be paid for. The latter seemed increasingly attractive.

Nature conservation and agriculture also included a series of more concrete (and perhaps more realistic) recommendations. A number concerned the need for more and better conservation advice for farmers. It was also suggested that the owners or occupiers of sssis should be required to notify the Ministry of Agriculture or Department of Agriculture or the FC before carrying out any new management on sssis. In return the land would be exempt from Capital Transfer Tax (a provision introduced in the 1975 Finance Act), and the NCC should extend the use of Management Agreements under Section 15 of the 1968 Countryside Act 'to provide a financial incentive for owners to manage sssis so as to retain their scientific interest'. It was, the report argued 'manifestly unreasonable that owners and farmers should be expected to provide money or forego profit for the maintenance of wildlife habitats on behalf of the nation'. This view, which became known (and widely castigated) as 'the voluntary principle' in debate on the Wildlife and Countryside Bill in 1980, became law when the Act was passed in 1981. In 1977, the NCC thought that the cost of such agreements 'would be of the order of £2.5m per year', of which it could provide but a fraction out of its current budget. The balance, they explained mysteriously 'would have to be obtained in other ways'.

They clearly envisaged the possibility of obtaining money from other departments of government, perhaps from the agricultural budget itself. This idea, again, has resurfaced recently. The NCC saw room for similar co-operative approaches in the form of 'incentive or compensation payments' for conservation management in the wider countryside. These would include specific maintenance grants for specific features, general financial assistance and grants for creative conservation. There was discussion of the idea of declared 'conservation zones' where there were 'concentrations of good wildlife habitats'. This was, of course, an attempt to resuscitate the Huxley Committee 'Scientific Areas', and it was rapidly found to be unpopular. It was replaced in the actual recommendations of the report with an earlier call for co-operative grant aid with the CC, FC and Crofters Commission to provide grants to further conservation management where compatible with other uses.

Nature conservation and agriculture raised a number of issues which remained high on the agenda of debate. The most fundamental was the question of whether agriculture and conservation could coexist. Words like consensus, flexibility, encouragement and education were used liberally, most notably by the Countryside Review Committee (CRC) which was set up by the Department of the Environment in 1974 as a talking shop on the English and Welsh Countryside. In 1976 they published *The countryside: problems and policies*. This stressed the need for consensus, perhaps the most overworked and distinctively British concept in conservation. The idea that this was a way forward was fostered by the leaflet put out by the NFU and Country Landowners' Association (CLA) in 1977 *Caring for the countryside*, a response to the NCC's report. In 1978 the CRC produced another topic paper, *Food production in the countryside*. This was clear about the problem: 'we have a situation where for the first time in our history there is an increasing divergence between farming on the one hand and landscape and amenity conservation on the other: and the farmer, far from being accepted as the guardian of the countryside, is in danger of being regarded as its potential destroyer'.

The following February, the government produced a new White Paper, *Farming and the nation*, which recognised the growing conflict between conservation and agriculture, but was skillfuly equivocal about what should be done. It called again for an impossible balance in similar terms to those of the 1968 Act: 'A balance therefore has to be struck. The government will continue to give a high priority to conserving the natural beauty of the countryside, while equally having regard to the needs of agriculture and forestry and the economic and social interests of rural areas'. The argument that agricultural development and conservation were pulling in completely different directions had apparently not sunk in. The government did agree to look at the CRC proposals that the Agricultural Development and Advisory Service might be more closely involved in countryside affairs, and the White Paper praised 'joint initiatives' by farmers and conservationists. It argued that some capital grant applications had been refused or schemes modified where 'in certain special cases' the Agriculture Minister had acted with 'regard for the desirability of conserving the countryside' as required by the 1968 Act.

These platitudes did little to clear the muddy waters, although they did represent an advance on MAFF's former position. One reason for this might be the presentation to Parliament in December 1978 of a new Countryside Bill by the then Labour government. This was 'to amend law relating to the conversion into agricultural land of moor and heath in National Parks ... and otherwise to amend the law relating to National Parks and the countryside'. Ten years after the 1968 Act, significantly stronger legislation was being introduced. The main stimulus came from the general countryside conservation side, not nature conservation, and in particular the criticism of the national parks system in a report by Lord Sandford in 1974.

The background is complex, and is described in detail by Ann and Malcolm McEwen in their book *National Parks: conser-*

vation or cosmetics? Problems began in the 1960s, when the County National Parks Committees found themselves powerless to prevent the reclamation of key areas of land within the Exmoor National Park. The Exmoor Society mapped the shrinking moorland in 1966, and the NFU and CLA reacted strongly to what they saw as exaggeration in the resulting report. The 1968 Countryside Act did not give powers to stop moorland reclamation, which of course was grant-aided by MAFF, and in the mid-1970s a series of areas were reclaimed. The management agreements which could be offered by the National Park Committee were too low to attract farmers voluntarily. The committee failed to prevent reclamation and in May 1977 were reported to the Secretary of State by the CC for mishandling the situation. In April, Lord Porchester was appointed to study the problem.

His work confirmed the disputed figures for moorland loss (his data are shown in Fig. 3.6), and he proposed that the National Park Authority should be empowered to make a Moorland Conservation Order 'to prevent such operations and practices as are likely to alter the vegetation or the general character of moorland to any material degree'. The nub of his proposal was that a farmer whose freedom to develop his land was restricted by a moorland conservation order should receive compensation. He held that this should be a once-for-all capital payment to reflect the reduction in land value, not an annual payment based on loss of profits as the NFU and expert valuers' suggested. On top of this, conservation grants should be introduced to further positive management desired by the national parks authority 'sufficiently generous to be attractive to the farmers concerned'.

These proposals were in line with the NCC's view that farmers should be compensated if restrained because of conservation. The question of how compensation should be calculated was left open. In 1978 the CRC had proposed 'a voluntary and flexible policy, based on advice, encouragement, education and financial inducements', which they hoped would win 'the broad support of the farming community itself'. The NFU made representations to the NCC in March 1979 about the difficulties caused when MAFF refused grand aid on SSSIs, and in their Fifth Report the NCC repeated their conviction 'that farmers and landowners should receive compensation if it is decided in the national interest that

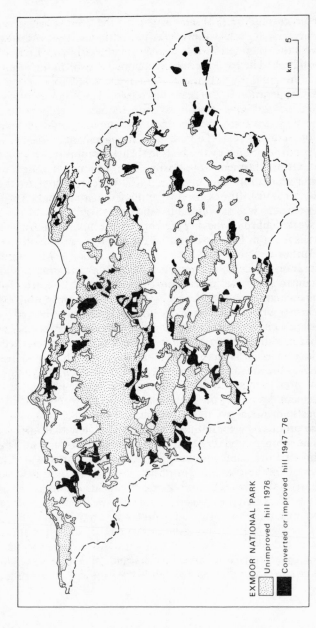

EXMOOR NATIONAL PARK

Unimproved hill 1976

Converted or improved hill 1947–76

Figure 3.6 The conversion of moorland on Exmoor between 1947 and 1976.

any of their land should be managed for conservation'. This requirement, that farmers should not lose at all from the designation of their land, implied that payments should be made on the basis of the profits which might have been made each year if development had gone ahead. This was exactly what the NFU wanted, and what Porchester had rejected.

The 1978/79 Countryside Bill was an attempt to put Lord Porchester's ideas onto the statute book. They were too much for the Conservative opposition, who objected strongly to both its detail, and the principles behind it. In the January debate, Michael Allison MP said of the moorland conservation orders 'the Minister has brought forward an unsatisfactory Bill. We like parts of it, but we are profoundly opposed to the compulsion element'. Edward Du Cann MP (with a Somerset constituency) argued of the Exmoor proposals 'the Bill is badly drafted, ill-considered, negative and unnecessary. That is a fact, not opinion. It is not the way forward for Exmoor, it is rather the way back'. He believed the Bill 'represents an unprecedented system of legal controls in peacetime on the farmer's traditional freedom to pursue his farming policies in accordance with his circumstances'. Michael Jopling MP, also a Conservative and later (in 1985) Minister of Agriculture, said 'the way forward lies in the creation of more management agreements'. The message comes through quite clearly: farmers must be paid for conservation. This was the farmers' view, and it was apparently shared by most Conservative MPs, and indeed by the NCC itself.

The Countryside Bill failed when the Labour government fell in the election of June 1979. However, the new government was also committed to conservation legislation. The difference now was that the government view of the right way to link farming and conservation was in line with that of the farmers themselves. The stage was set for the Wildlife and Countryside Bill, and a battle royal on conservation.

Further reading

Abercrombie, P. 1933. *Town and country planning.* Oxford: Oxford University Press.

Barton, P. M. and G. P. Buckley 1983. The status and protection of notified sites of special scientific interest in south-east England. *Biol. Conserv.* 27, 213–42.

HMSO 1975. *Food from our own resources.* Cmnd 6020. London: HMSO.

HMSO 1979. *Farming and the nation.* Cmnd 7458. London: HMSO.

Lowe, P. D. and J. M. Goyder 1983. *Environmental groups in politics.* London: Allen & Unwin.

MacEwan, A. and M. MacEwan 1982. *National parks: conservation or cosmetics?* London: Allen & Unwin.

Mabey, R. 1980. *Common ground.* London: Hutchinson.

Nature Conservancy Council 1977. *Nature conservation and agriculture.* London: Nature Conservancy Council.

Ratcliffe, D. A. (ed.) 1977. *A nature conservation review,* Cambridge University Press.

Sharp, T. 1940. *Town planning.* Harmondsworth: Penguin.

Sheail, J. 1985. *Pesticides and nature conservation: the British experience.* Oxford: Oxford University Press.

Street, A. G. 1932. *Farmers' glory.* London: Faber and Faber.

Chapter Four

The Wildlife
and Countryside Act

The Bill in perspective

The newly elected Conservative government announced on 20 June 1979 that it intended to introduce a Wildlife and Countryside Bill. In part it was already committed to introducing legislation on the countryside to follow the previous government's Countryside Bill, but a further need to ratify the 1979 EEC Birds directive by 1981 led to a much broader – and much longer – piece of legislation. By August 1979 the first of a series of six consultation papers had been produced by the DOE proposing a range of measures concerning the countryside, and these began over a year of controversy and intensive lobbying on all sides.

By the time the Bill was actually introduced to Parliament in November 1980, it was clear that it was a measure over which there was deep political controversy. Conservation legislation has rarely been so divisive, but the Bill was still apparently expected to be fairly straightforward because it went first to the House of Lords where greater expertise in countryside matters is conventionally supposed to reside. In fact the Bill's introduction was delayed and it eventually remained with Parliament for 11 months, and was subject to a phenomenal 2300 amendments, very few of them (such being the strength of the government's majority) being upheld.

It would be a worthy project to collect and publish the debates, for they are at the same time the best and the worst of British democracy at work: there was much debate, for example, about the difference in aggression between beef bulls and dairy bulls and the safety of ramblers on footpaths, remarkably informed discussion (in the Lords of course) about whether birds like the bar-tailed godwit, the bean goose or the scaup should be protected, and some fairly abstruse debate about other issues. The question of Sunday wildfowling, for example, was given close attention: it was already banned in Scotland, most of Wales and parts of England, and Lord Melchett moved an amendment suggesting standardisation. Let wildfowlers and birdwatchers share the weekend. Not so, said the Earl of Swinton, far better for the birdwatchers to have the birds up and flying around, disturbed by shot, than 'all tucked away in the reedbeds and marshes'.

Hansard is a rich source of peppery and revealing comments on most aspects of the long debate, but although it records the debates verbatim, these are but the tip of the iceberg as regards what was really happening during the passage of the Bill. Until some of those involved publish their diaries (if indeed they had the time to write them) we will be left guessing about exactly what was being planned, what fierce debates went on behind the scenes, and who was putting pressure on whom. None the less, the bare bones of the debate are clear, indeed its course largely followed the lines set out in preceding years.

The Wildlife and Countryside Bill has three parts. The first concerns the protection of individual species: it sets out what species can and cannot be shot or taken, and in what circumstances, updating and replacing the Protection of Birds Act 1954 and the Wild Creatures and Wild Plants Act 1975. The third section covers access to the countryside, footpaths and rights in the countryside. Both of these enjoyed some measure of controversy, both provoking sharp exchanges between landowners and countryside users, plus their share of letters to the press. Neither approached the level of controversy achieved by Part II of the Bill which concerned the conservation of natural habitats and open moorland. In this area conservationists, landowners (and Parliament) were already fully sensitised to the issue of whether it was necessary to restrict the freedom of landowners and farmers in the name of conservation, and how it could reasonably be done. The Parliamentary debate of the Bill brought these issues to a head, and ended, possibly for good, the notion that nature conservation and intensive agriculture or forestry are not essentially in conflict.

Consultation

Controversy over the questions raised by the Wildlife and Countryside Bill predates the Parliamentary debate by over a year, although it is there that it is most clearly recorded. If one had to point to the single most significant impact of the Bill on conservation, it would probably not be its actual provisions (although these are very important), but its galvanising – and radicalising – effect on conservation bodies, particularly the 'non-governmental organisations' (NGOs) like the RSPB and RSNC. They entered the debates in 1979 rather innocent and certainly inexperienced politically, and found their feet, and a co-ordinated voice the hard way. The Labour Peer, Lord Melchett, called together a group called 'Wildlife Link' in the autumn of 1979 to co-ordinate the nature conservation case and put pressure on the NCC. This included almost all the organisations concerned in wildlife and nature conservation, the RSPB, RSNC, FOE, the Underwater Conservation Society (now Marine Conservation Society) and many others. For the first time there was the chance of a clear and united independent conservation voice.

It was raised most strongly to counter the sophisticated and effective lobbying of the landowners' and farmers' organisation, the Country Landowners' Association (CLA) and the National Farmers' Union (NFU). These two, often referred to rather perjoritively as 'the farming lobby', had of course long ago learned the advantages of co-ordination, and were experienced at political lobbying. They already had the staff and organisation to catch important ears in both Westminster and Whitehall, and by mid-1979 were hard at work putting over their views about compensation, management agreements, moorland conservation orders and SSSIs.

Their assiduousness, and their expertise, won them early

discussion not only with the MAFF but with DOE before the discussion papers were produced. These came from DOE's rural directorate, but unbelievably they were not discussed with either the NCC or the CC. Probably as a result, they represented a substantial withdrawal from the position of the Labour Countryside Bill, and recommended very weak powers of habitat protection. The papers on habitat protection, and on moorland, went against the recommendations of Porchester and suggested no powers to make conservation orders. Moorland areas of SSSIs would be conserved by voluntary agreement with farmers, if necessary in the form of formal management agreements. This 'voluntary approach' represented no advance on the existing powers which had been proven on Exmoor and in SSSIs to be inadequate. It was exactly the approach favoured by the NFU and CLA since it placed farmers in a controlling position and placed no restrictions on their rights and privileges.

The consultation paper *Conservation of Habitats* did make some small extra provision for SSSIs. It proposed that the Secretary of State should designate 'a small number of selected sites' where landowners or tenants would be legally obliged (subject to penalty) 'to give 12 months' notice to the NCC of their intention to undertake practices which could be detrimental to these identified scientific interest'. This was a poor provision – it meant that in a small number of cases (the number of only 40 of the 3500 SSSIs was talked about informally) it would be possible for the secretary of state to prevent damage to SSSIs for the period of a year. All other SSSIs were left unprotected. These 'super-SSSIs' themselves would not be chosen by the NCC, and there were no new powers to persuade a landowner or tenant to manage the site for conservation. If they rejected a management agreement, the only resort was compulsory purchase, a cumbersome, unpopular and almost never-used procedure which contained no safeguard against the vindictive destruction of the special interest of the land in question.

One might have expected that given their concern about SSSI loss the NCC would refuse to accept this half-measure. There were two grounds on which they might question the proposal: first that it was unreasonable to limit protection to only a tiny percentage of SSSIs, and secondly that if such a limited target were accepted that it should be the NCC and not the Secretary of State which selected the sites. In fact, they hesitated, then cautiously tackled the second point. In September the chairman wrote to the Secretary of State applauding 'the firm statement of the Government's duty to wildlife resources', but advising that they themselves should draw up the list of key sites. They also suggested that 'in the interests of relations with landowners and occupiers' only three months was needed to assess the impact of damaging operations. Their meekness won them no ground: the Secretary of State assured them that their advice on sites would be called upon, but argued that designation implied 'a government commitment to protection, and the Government must therefore take all relevant factors into account, including resources, before deciding to afford such protection'. After further discussion with DOE officials in November, the Council wrote again welcoming the proposals, merely asking that sites should only be designated by the Secretary of State following representation by the NCC.

This early acquiescence by the NCC had a cathartic effect on the whole debate about the Act, because they were alone on the conservation side in viewing the DOE's proposals as adequate. The CC, backed by amenity groups, tried through the autumn of 1979 to persuade the NCC to adopt a common front calling for more extensive designations and the provision for a ministerial 'stop order' if a management agreement could not be concluded. This was too much for the NCC, who would not co-operate, and it was not until the end of 1980 that sustained lobbying by Wildlife Link caused them to reverse their policy. By then it was almost too late.

The NCC's difficulty was twofold. First, and most fundamentally, it was at this time a deeply conservative body. However concerned and radical (and experienced) the professional officers were, decisions were taken by the appointed Council. A number of the councilors were elderly and all were respectable, establishment figures, including landowners with an interest in nature, most of them deeply conservative both about interfering with landowners' rights in land and about jeopardising the goodwill and co-operation which they believed formed the basis of conservation in the countryside. Some had direct interests in farming or forestry, which inevitably coloured their view, and there was great commitment to the landowners' comforting concept of 'stewardship', as a burden nobly borne on behalf of society. They were extremely cautious about standing up to the obvious will of the government they were called upon to advise. Secondly, although they were rapidly to discover how sincerely conservationists in the voluntary body disagreed with them, they were simply following their own policies on key sites to a logical conclusion.

Perhaps in despair at the apparent impossibility of protecting all SSSIS, the NCC had moved towards the concept of grading sites in Britain in terms of their importance. In retrospect this seems a tactical blunder of some magnitude, since by classifying one site as of lower value than another it makes the former almost impossible to protect, either in terms of demanding resources to buy it, or asking other agencies to respect it. If a site is Grade 2 it is obviously not of the first importance, so why worry? For political reasons, judged crucial at the time, this approach was used in the national review of sites, *A nature conservation review*. This was finished by 1970, but its publication was delayed until 1977 partly because of fears about the political implications of a published 'shopping list'. A total of almost 1 million ha of land was described, and the inclusion of quite large areas for the first time, particularly in the uplands, may certainly have been sensitive. To reduce the shock effect, and to fudge the fact that it was in effect a bid for 735 NNRs, it was stressed that the sites were simply of *equivalent quality* to NNRs. The 735 sites were classified as Grade 1, which were 'of national importance' and Grade 2 of 'almost equal' importance but whose conservation was 'of less extreme urgency'. Below this, 'ordinary' SSSIS were further classified as either Grade 3 (of regional importance) and Grade 4 (of county importance). This graded system was intended to make the NCC's site protection policy both more comprehensible, and less frightening and offensive. At the same time, Derek Ratcliffe, NCC's chief scientist, commented in the introduction that 'the national strategy for nature conservation must consist of much more than the safeguarding of a hard core of key sites'.

The grading of sites may have seemed a way of making the preservation of the best sites more possible. However, many conservationists saw it instead as meaning that it would be harder than ever to protect the 'average' SSSI because it would always be seen to be less than the best. In the event, the DOE's 'super-SSSI' concept was merely an extension of the NCC's own key site approach. It is perhaps then unsurprising that the NCC did not stand up to the DOE, but accepted with so little fuss the principle that only a handful even of their NCR 'key sites' would receive extra protection. It is unsurprising also, given their support in 1975 and again subsequently for the notion of voluntary management agreements with farmers, that they shrank away from the suggestion that the DOE proposals were not strong enough.

Two events, backed up by sustained lobbying from the voluntary bodies, caused the NCC to more or less reverse their policy. First, the NCC produced some new figures of habitat loss which may have stiffened the Council's resolve. Certainly the figures were alarming: in 1980, 8% of SSSIs notified for their biological interest had been damaged, out of a total of 235 sites, and at a minimum 5700 ha was affected. Damage in some counties was higher than this, 32% of sites in Dorset and 22% in Gloucestershire being affected for example. A random sample of 443 SSSIs was therefore taken and 399 of them were visited in 1980. Fifty-nine had suffered damage: 13% of the whole sample or almost 15% of those visited. Of these 30 (51%) had been damaged by agricultural operations (drainage, ploughing, fertiliser or pesticide application) or the ending of traditional management such as grazing. The NCC concluded in their Seventh Report 'However the results of these surveys are interpreted, it is evident that damage to SSSIs is considerable and has reached a level that gives concern not only to the NCC but to all those who are interested in the future of Britain's natural heritage'.

The second event which influenced the NCC was the acceptance by Parliament in August 1980 of streamlined procedures of farm capital grant approvals. Following the Rayner Review, grants were now to be approved retrospectively (i.e. after work had been done). To protect the nature conservation interest, farmers wishing to carry out work on SSSIs for which they required grants would have to consult the NCC first. This new principle gave the NCC hope that they could ask for similar provision on all SSSIs. Lord Melchett addressed a Council meeting in November 1980, and in the words of the Seventh Annual Report 'we concluded that further measures to protect all SSSIs should be written into the Bill during its passage through Parliament' (p. 45). The chairman therefore wrote to the Secretary of State asking for a government amendment to require prior notification by farmers on all SSSIs, but to no avail. On 12 December the NCC finally – a year late as most conservationists saw it – made their dissatisfaction with this and other aspects of the Bill quite clear in a press statement. By that time the Bill's long passage through Parliament had already begun.

The debate in Parliament

The Wildlife and Countryside Bill was introduced to Parliament on 25 November 1980. It incorporated a number of amendments suggested through the consultation process, but still offered advanced notification of damage to only a handful of 'super SSSIs'. Ian Prestt, director of the RSPB, wrote in *Birds* that he had 'mixed feelings' about the Bill: it was 'good in parts but disturbingly bad in others'. The director of the CPRE was more forthright. He said simply 'the Bill has no teeth'. The Bill went first to the Lords, had its second Reading on 16 December, and was then debated in detail in a committee of the whole house in January and February 1981.

Seven amendments were carried against the government in the Lords, although interestingly none of these was strongly opposed by 'the farming lobby,' and of those which *were* so opposed, none were passed. The most interesting of the successful amendments was that moved by the Rev. Lord Sandford to allow MAFF to make grants for conservation, recreation, tourism or craft industry, or otherwise to develop the rural economy. This was narrowly won, and excited observers at the time because it opened the way to making MAFF manage the countryside as 'a socioeconomic totality and not a food-factory' as Chris Hall put it in *Vole* magazine. He also commented 'of all the Government's defeats in the Lords this is the one Ministers are most likely to want to reverse in the more whippable Commons'.

From the point of view of nature conservation, the debate over SSSI protection was much more important and here there was no success, despite a radical change in the background to the whole debate. This was provided by the timely publication of Marion Shoard's book *The theft of the countryside* in October. This powerfully polemical study of the effects of modern agriculture on the countryside rapidly generated a storm of controversy in the national press and media. It was reviewed kindly by *The Times* and a long correspondence ensued, while the evidence and the implications were widely discussed. Marion Shoard asked for agriculture to be subject to planning control, and almost over-night she blew the whole question of agriculture and conser-vation wide open.

Perhaps even more telling in its way was the announcement by the NCC of new evidence of SSSI loss. As the government's advisors on conservation, the disparity between their data on the rapid rate of damage to sites and the government's refusal to introduce stronger measures to protect them was obvious, and politically embarassing. The NCC's evidence to the House of Lords Select Committee on Science and Technology in June 1980 showed that between 30% and 50% of Britain's ancient broadleaved woodland had been lost since 1947, and other studies showed a 21% reduction in the area of chalk grassland since 1960 and the loss of wildlife interest in 8% of Oxfordshire floodplain meadows over the preceding two years alone. The *Sunday Times* carried a full page article by Brian Jackson on habitat loss in December 1980, FOE published *Paradise lost* in the spring. The figures were highlighted by David Goode, assistant chief scientist of the NCC, in his article in *New Scientist* on 22 January. On 11 February, the NCC issued a press release, citing the particular case of Horton Common SSSI. Between December 1980 and February 1981, while the Bill was being debated in the Lords, all but 30 ha of 134 ha of heathland at Horton Common in Dorset was rotovated for conversion to pasture after the NCC and voluntary bodies had failed to conclude a management agreement or persuade the owner to sell. The site was destroyed, the measures to preserve it patently inadequate, and the NCC said so in its press release. The case received national newspaper, tele-vision and radio coverage, and earned the NCC a hot rebuke from the Minister of Agriculture.

Despite this publicity, and the NCC's own urgings, the government refused to support an amendment in the Lords which would extend protection to all SSSIs: it was defeated by 109 votes to 100. Chris Hall comments 'the protection (or non-protection) of SSSIs was one of the three great cruxes of the Bill and perhaps that on which the Government's determination to employ no teeth against farmers and landowners was most evident'. What was wanted by both the NCC and the voluntary bodies was a requirement that farmers should notify the NCC of potentially damaging operations on *all* SSSIs. The voluntary bodies also felt that the NCC should have the power to make an order forbidding such operations. The NCC believed that if they were given enough financial resources to offer management agreements then a limited period of prohibition would be enough. An enforcing order by the Secretary of State would only then be needed if negotiations broke down. In the event nothing was done to protect all SSSIs. The NCC was given the duty to inform owners and occupiers of the scientific interest of sites, and the nature of operations which would be damaging, and in response to the revelation about SSSI loss the government proposed a voluntary code of guidance for SSSIs. Both of these were sensible provisions, but neither contributed much to the basic problem of habitat and SSSI loss. The NCC chairman argued in a letter to the Secretary of State in March that no voluntary code could be 'effective in restraining either that minority of farmers who care nothing for conservation or those who feel, in the present economic circumstances that they have no option but to maximise production'.

The publicity given to the data on SSSI loss and the government's failure to move away from the 'voluntary principle' made for jaundiced views of the Bill on the part of many conservationists. Thus Max Nicholson, former Director-General of the NCC, wrote in the *Guardian* in March 1981 'having dodged since mid-century the issue of national land use planning, the Government lacks any basis of responding to the issue other than giving in to the strongest pressure group'. He was in no doubt that this group was the landowning lobby. The Bill reached the Commons in April. In his speech introducing the Bill the Secretary of State endorsed the voluntary principle strongly. 'There were', he said, 'two broad options about how to secure the regime for the countryside disciplines we seek. The first is the compulsory one.

The second is to seek an established standard of conduct that leaves the owner to proceed. We have chosen the latter course in Clause 28. In moving the second Reading of the Bill I should make clear the Government's attitude in this aspect. We are not prepared, as a Government, to support amendments that would change this basic approach. In our view, the cause of conservation is done no good by using compulsion as the primary means of making landowners and farmers manage their land for the general benefit of our heritage'.

The Bill was read in the Commons, then sent to a Standing Commitee away from the limelight and where voting was very much on party lines. Over 930 amendments were tabled although not all were discussed. The Sandford amendment was removed, to be replaced with an anodyne clause requiring the Minister of Agriculture to consider the aims of conservation, but 'only in so far as may be consistent with the agricultural purposes of a scheme'. However, the Bill was pushing perilously close to the end of the Parliamentary session, and the Labour Opposition was known to be prepared to talk it out of time rather than see the Bill go through unamended. The government made concessions: limestone pavements were protected, and more importantly a statutory requirement was placed on owners and occupiers who wanted to carry out potentially damaging operations on an SSSI to first notify the NCC. The NCC had argued strongly for this in a letter to the Secretary of State, and in an all-party briefing document to MPs. It seemed to offer the only way of preventing a farmer from going ahead on his own without grant aid with operations like drainage which would damage an SSSI. However, other amendments passed in Committee were less immediately favourable for conservation: before new SSSIs could be established owners would have the statutory right to be consulted, and (arguably most damaging of all) the NCC was required to compensate farmers if an agricultural grant were refused on conservation grounds. In the long run this last provision may prove a benefit in disguise (indeed, one view classes it as a deliberate ploy), because it forced the government to bear directly the cost of conservation, which may in the end make the adoption of cheaper and more effective measures more likely.

This last provision satisfied the NFU and CLA, but sent spasms of alarm through the ranks of conservationists as its implications sunk in. It was one of the issues hotly debated when the Standing Committee's amendments were considered by the Commons in July. The NCC argued that the existing proposals for SSSIs were inadequate, and that a three-month notification of damaging operations was required. This was one of the areas strengthened in the Commons, but the clause about compensation remained. Attempts were made to remove it when the Bill was debated again in the Lords in October 1981. An amendment was tabled by Lord Buxton and Lord Onslow to make the offer of a management agreement optional and not compulsory for the NCC (and in national parks the county planning authorities). But, crucially, the NCC failed to back it because the element of compulsion did two important things, it removed the element of uncertainty which had bedevilled negotiations between the conservation agencies and farmers and landowners in the past, and it meant that the government had to give the NCC the money to pay the compensation. In the Commons in July, the government had promised to meet its commitment to conservation, 'as far as possible within such resources as are available'. Also, it must be said, the NCC had gone on record over preceding years as supporting the principle that farmers should be paid if they had to forego the right to develop land in the name of conservation. In the Lords the vote on the Buxton–Craigton amendment was taken: it was defeated by two votes only, 57 for, 59 against. Management agreements were to be mandatory.

That was the end of the fireworks. The Bill went back to the Commons briefly on 29 October, and finally received Royal Assent on 30 October 1981. The Wildlife and Countryside Act was on the statute books, and had been debated at great length, yet its implications for conservation were far from clear. The swift amendments in the Commons had produced a Bill whose detailed provisions were far from well worked out. While its fine complexities took time to appear, some problems were only too immediately apparent. Ann and Malcolm MacEwen, writing in *The Planner* in May 1982, noted 'that ministers have sold Parliament a pig-in-a-poke. They refused to say precisely what the principles of compensation would be or to indicate how much money the Government would provide to enable the conservation authorities to pay the compensation'. This compensation element was judged by some potentially disastrous. The MacEwens believed 'the Wildlife and Countryside Act 1981 is, quite literally, unprincipled. It is a dead end, from which another government will have to retreat before it can advance by a different route. It leaves agriculture and conservation on a collision course, but provides no way of regulating the conflict except by pouring small amounts of money into a bottomless pit' (p. 71). This was one of many critical views of the new Act. Before seeing how valid such criticism has been, we need to look first at exactly what provisions the Act finally incorporated for the protection of nature conservation sites.

The Act in practice

Despite the breadth and detail of debate about the Wildlife and Countryside Bill, or possibly because of it, the Act itself is a complex piece of legislation. In the last four years it has lost none of the controversy attached to the original Bill, indeed as the cumbersome and bureaucratic nature of its provision for SSSI protection and the soaring cost of management agreements came to the notice of observers the criticism increased. For some conservationists, disillusionment with the Act has been complete. Two quite separate Private Member's Bills have gone before Parliament to try to close important loopholes, while a separate Bill was passed in July 1985 to cover a technicality left unclear by the Act's hard-pressed draughtsmen in their haste to encompass amendments in 1981.

The Wildlife and Countryside Act runs to 74 sections and 17 Schedules. Its preamble says simply that it is 'an Act to repeal and re-enact with amendments the Protection of Birds Act 1954 to 1967 and the Conservation of Wild Creatures and Wild Plants Act 1975; ... to amend the law relating to nature conservation, the countryside and National Parks ...' The significant piece of the Act in this respect is Part II, Sections 28 to 52. Sections 28 and 29 directly concern SSSIs, and together they are a massive 25 paragraphs long. Section 28 requires the NCC to notify the local planning authority, every owner and occupier, and the Secretary of State of each SSSI, specifying which features are of scientific interest and the nature of any operations likely to damage that interest. The owner or occupier may not then carry out one of these operations unless he has given written notice of his intention to do so to the NCC and they have either given their written consent, or agreed to the operation under a management agreement, or until three months have elapsed since notice was given. A small fine (originally set in 1981 at £500) is payable if he does so. However, if the work can be construed an emergency operation and if the NCC is notified as soon as practicable afterwards, or if the operation is covered by planning permission, he can go ahead before the end of the three month period. If he does not accept a management agreement, he can go ahead with the damaging operation when the three months are elapsed anyway.

This is complicated, but what it does is essentially to guarantee a breathing space before a site is damaged by any operation (including agriculture) while the NCC tries to persuade the owner or occupier to accept a management agreement which will compensate him for not developing the site. This is certainly a gain, although a small one, since – as experience was rapidly to prove – three months was a perilously short period to bring a reluctant occupier to the point of accepting a management agreement, while a kindly-disposed farmer hardly needed to be constrained by the heavy-handed procedure. Against this, there was some helpful clarification about SSSIs, which were now to be registered as a land charge (so a solicitor's search would reveal them) and were to be notified unambiguously to all owners and occupiers for the first time. Ironically, this extra information led to abuse. Paragraph 2 allowed a three month period for consultation before any new SSSI could be established: this rapidly became controversial as it became clear that some reluctant owners and occupiers were taking the opportunity to damage sites. Strenuous efforts were made in 1984 and 1985 to change this provision in the form of Private Members' Bills to amend the 1981 Act. These are described in more detail in Chapter 5.

As it was passed, however, Section 28 was obviously weak. Two things strengthen it. One was the power to make a nature conservation order (NCO) under Section 29, the other the nature of the management agreements which the NCC was bound by

Section 32 to offer those farmers refused capital grant. As Malcolm MacEwen commented, the Act itself does not specify the basis for those agreements, leaving that to the separate (and undebated) Financial Guidelines published for the first time in September 1982. These were greeted with dismay by conservationists because they followed the pattern set on Exmoor in April 1981 by going against the Porchester Report and offering an alternative between a once-off capital payment and a recurrent annual payment. Suffice it to say at this stage that the agreements were generous to farmers, and that this raised all sorts of problems about the overall cost of agreements on SSSIs, although it made the task of persuading farmers to accept them rather easier than it might have been otherwise.

The element of compulsion in Section 29 was more difficult. This gave the Secretary of State the power to make a nature conservation order preventing anyone (including obviously the owner) from carrying out a damaging operation on a particular SSSI. They could, however, give the NCC written notice of their intention to do so, in which case the NCC had three months to reply, either giving them written permission to proceed, or offering a management agreement. If the NCC failed to reply, the owner or occupier could go ahead. However, if an agreement was offered, there was a ban on the operation for a minimum of 12 months from the date of the first notification of intent to damage the site. This could be longer if negotiation trailed on before failing, but there was always three months grace between the collapse of negotiations and freedom to damage the site. In the case of a site protected by a Section 29 Order, anyone convicted of damage would be liable to a hefty fine (up to £1000 plus £100 a day if the offence continued) and to 'restoring the land to its former condition' (Section 31). On the other hand they would also, under Section 30, be eligible for compensation by the NCC for direct loss or damage or for 'expenditure rendered abortive' by the placing of the order.

Again, these provisions are complex. They provide a mechanism – albeit quite a cumbersome one – for protecting an SSSI for long enough for an intractable owner or occupier to be able to consider properly the offer of a management agreement. At the end of the day, however, all Section 29 does is to buy time: if the

107

owner steadfastly refuses an agreement, after a year he can go ahead without further hindrance. In that circumstance, the NCC's only sanction is to acquire the land by compulsory purchase: a power they have had since 1949, and rarely use because of its manifest potential for offending landowners. Viewed in this light, Section 29 is far from being a guarantee of the safety of SSSIs, the more so because the power to make the order is in the hands of the Secretary of State not the NCC, and because of the slightly equivocal nature in which the Act specifies *which* sites it may be applied to. According to paragraph 2, an Order can be made on any area 'of special interest' and 'national importance'. Does this mean *any* SSSI, (after all each is of 'special' interest and each is part of a national series) or is this the old idea of 'super-SSSIs' again? Differing interpretations of this point have made for a number of problems in the last four years.

Sections 28 and 29 are the crux of Part II of the Act as regards nature conservation, but there were other provisions. Section 31 covers the preparation of a code of guidance for SSSIs; Section 34 empowers the Secretary of State to make a Limestone Pavement Order forbidding the removal or disturbance of limestone (thus ending the rustling of limestone and its legal removal for the garden trade); Section 35 extends the NCC's freedom to declare NNRss to land held by other bodies and managed by them as a nature reserve; Sections 36 and 37 allow the establishment of Marine Nature Reserves (a subject of considerable controversy both in debate over the Bill and subsequently); Section 38 gives the NCC far greater freedom to offer grants or loans to anyone 'doing anything which, in their opinion, is conducive to nature conservation or fostering the understanding of nature conservation'. Section 32 contains the vestigial remains of the 'Sandford' amendment requiring the Minister of Agriculture 'to further the conservation of the flora, fauna, geological or physiographic features by reason of which the land is of special interest' where a grant appliction affects an SSSI. Section 41 also requires MAFF to include in their advice to 'persons carrying on an agricultural business' material on 'the conservation and enhancement of the natural beauty and amenity of the countryside'.

108

After the Act

The new Act came into force in stages. The principal sssi provisions and the sections covering limestone pavement orders and marine nature reserves came into force on 30 November 1981. Other parts had to wait for relevant commencement orders. Thus the potentially useful (if typically anodyne) requirement placed on water authorities and internal drainage boards to 'so exercise their functions with respect to the proposals as to further the conservation and enhancement of natural beauty and the conservation of flora, fauna and geological or physiographical features of special interest' (Section 48) waited until February 1982.

Even before the Act was passed, work had begun to fashion the Code of Guidance for sssis. This was done by the DOE, but a committee met with NCC present, as well as representation from MAFF, the FC, the Timber Growers of Great Britain Ltd., the NFU and the CLA. Until this point, forestry had been excluded from specific mention in the Act for fear of raising more concern in the Lords than could be usefully channelled into the legislation. This anomalous situation was only partially eased by the inclusion of some rather limited consideration of forestry in the Code of Guidance. The NCC later chose to extend the principle of the Act to forestry as well as agriculture. Draft guidelines were available by September 1981, and were published as a consultation document in March 1982 before being put to Parliament in July. The voluntary bodies were unanimous in condemning the guidelines as too weak and too woolly. They were approved by Parliament in October 1982, and published. They were described as 'an exercise in official cynicism' by FOE, and 'bland and cynical' by John Andrews of the RSPB. He wrote 'instead of explaining that an sssi ought to be a source of pride for a landowner, it concentrates on the administrative procedures for objecting to the creation of sssis and for claiming compensation'. Meanwhile the NFU and CLA were stressing the moral responsibilities attached to tenure of an sssi as part of a determined campaign to make a success of the 'voluntary principle'. Barry Denyer-Green, who wrote the chartered surveyors' handbook on the Act likened the guidelines to the Highway Code, admonishing but not restraining. It was not an auspicious start.

Controversy over the Act deepened when the draft *Financial Guidelines for management agreements* were circulated in September and their implications sank in. They were drafted by the DOE, MAFF and the Welsh Office, without any input from the NCC or other conservation bodies, and they were widely judged a disaster. In November the CPRE and the Council for National Parks argued in a report *The price of conservation* that they were of questionable legal and constitutional status because their detailed provisions had never been debated in Parliament. In a letter to the House of Commons Select Committee on the Environment asking them to investigate, they wrote: 'in their present form the Guidelines are inconsistent, unclear and, arguably, designed to operate beyond the scope prescribed in the Act itself. Moreover, if fully implemented as they stand, we believe they would prove impossibly expensive for conservation authorities, as well as hugely and expensively burdensome in administrative terms'. The chief objections to the guidelines were first that they were to be binding on conservation agencies, i.e. the figures specified were not guides on which to base agreements but were a definitive and compulsory basis for agreements which left little room for discretion. Secondly, they offered an annual payment on the basis of profit foregone, which opened the way to substantial index-linked annual expenditure by the NCC.

Despite opposition from conservation organisations, the guidelines were published in January 1983 substantially unchanged. The yawning gulf between the amount of money available to pay for management agreements and their likely cost received increasingly sharp critical attention: in March 1983 Chris Rose and Charles Secrett wrote *Cash or crisis*, a critical report which hammered the discrepancy home. They argued that the Act was failing to prevent the destruction and damage of SSSIS. This theme was taken up again by the Wildlife Link Habitats Working Group in November in a report which enumerated instances of site loss and damage.

Criticisms of this sort were voiced from a number of quarters through 1984 and 1985. As this is being written in July 1985, there is something of a lull in the debate about conservation, but the storm will resume. When it does, two questions will be paramount. How effective can the 1981 legislation actually be in controlling habitat loss? What kind of direction must we look to for improved policies? These questions are tackled in the last three chapters of this book, first looking at the Act and site protection, second looking at the cost of conservation, and lastly looking to the future.

Further reading

Adams, W. M. 1984. *Implementing the Act: a study of habitat protection under Part II of the Wildlife and Countryside Act 1981.* Oxford: British Association of Nature Conservationists and the World Wildlife Fund.

Cox, G. and P. D. Lowe 1983. A battle not the war: the politics of the Wildlife and Countryside Act. In *Countryside planning yearbook 1983*, A. W. Gilg (ed.), pp. 48–76. Norwich: Geo Books.

Denyer-Green, B. 1983. *The Wildlife and Countryside Act 1981: the practitioner's companion.* London: Surveyor's Publications.

MacEwan, A. and M. MacEwan 1982. An unprincipled Act? *The Planner* May/June, 69–71.

Rose, C. and C. Secrett 1982. *Cash or crisis: the imminent failure of the Wildlife and Countryside Act.* London: Friends of the Earth and the British Association of Nature Conservationists.

O'Riordan, T. 1983. Putting trust in the countryside. In *The conservation and development programme for the UK*, (ed.) The UK Conservation and development programme organising committee, pp. 171–260. London: Kogan page.

Shoard, M. 1980. *The theft of the countryside.* London: Temple Smith.

Chapter Five

The sssi system

Renotification

The key to the implementation of the sssi provisions of the Wildlife and Countryside Act is the duty laid on the ncc to notify owners and occupiers, plus the Secretary of State and planning authorities, of the nature of the site's special interest. Until the 1981 Act there was no legal need for the ncc to inform owners or occupiers, although of course in many cases they did so. There is a slight confusion over the different procedures involved with sssis already scheduled under the provisions of the 1949 National Parks and Access to the Countryside Act and new sites being included in the sssi series for the first time. The Act called for a clean sweep of the whole system, and whatever relations were with the owner or occupier, every existing sssi had to be properly notified: in the terminology of the ncc, each site was to be renotified. New sites, however, are said simply to be notified. The two procedures of renotification and notification are somewhat different (the latter being more complicated), but are confusingly, and inelegantly known jointly as '(re)notification'.

The whole process of notification and renotification has turned out to be extremely complex and time consuming, and fraught with procedural difficulty. It is quite clear that this was not fully foreseen either by those debating the proposed legislation in Parliament or indeed the ncc itself. Early estimates put the completion of the whole process at the end of 1983, but by March 1983 a reply to a Parliamentary question put the target back to the end of 1985. The NCC's 9th Report (1982–3) spoke of the process 'extending into 1986 in some areas' while the latest (1985) figures show that substantial completion would not be achieved at present rates of progress until 1987 or 1988, and even, in some areas, 1989. It would be quite wrong to see this slippage as a function of slackness on the part of the NCC: indeed when a cost-cutting 'Rayner Review' was done in 1983 on the NCC it (surprisingly) praised the workaholics in the regional offices labouring under the mountainous bureaucracy of renotification. The truth is that the task has been a lot larger and more complicated than was at first realised, certainly by those outside the NCC. Eventually, money was found to employ more staff, and the rate of work increased, but the task remains formidable. The reasons for its complexity are discussed below, and the progress made to date – as well as the prospects – are analysed in some detail. In passing it is simply important to record that – like the labours of Hercules – the task which seemed simple has proved most onerous.

It is certainly clear that the magnitude of the problem was widely, probably universally, underestimated. This was due largely to two misapprehensions. First, the amount of knowledge within the NCC about SSSIs and the distribution and character of wildlife habitats was overestimated. Second, the real significance of the new provision for SSSIs were underestimated. The Act brought the SSSI system a long way towards the nature reserve. Relations with owners and occupiers were to be formalised, sometimes determined by management agreements, but always involving management within strict bounds set by the proscribed potentially damaging operations. This new status of SSSIs required far more information on each site than had previously been necessary, and in addition a careful internal approval system because of the potential financial implications of possible management agreements. The significance of this will become clear as the various procedures involved first in renotification then new notifications are outlined.

There is an ideal process through which each SSSI must go before it is formally renotified, although the detail varies between the three countries to some degree. Initially each statutory NCC Country Advisory Committee had extensive freedom, which they

113

used, to devise their own procedures. Gradually standardisation has been established from Great Britain headquarters both to meet the legal complexities as they are revealed, and because renotification has become such an issue as regards NCC's grant from government. The first steps involve detailed site survey, the collection of data in a standardised format on habitats and species and the validation of the scientific interest of the site. Validation is less curious than it sounds, because a number of existing sssis have either lost their original interest through damage or successional change, or else are no longer of sssi standard for some other reason. The 'clean sweep' demands that as far as possible every sssi meets standardised criteria and is of a quality defensible at a public inquiry. The guidelines for sssi selection were redefined in 1979, and are currently (1985) being revised again, but they basically attempt to set minimum standards of quality for the remaining examples of natural and semi-natural vegetation and animal populations, occurrences of rare and endangered plant and animal species and key geological features.

In England data on habitats and species are (in theory at least) collected for all sssis: in Scotland the data are necessarily more fragmentary for some sites, especially the large mountain sssis (e.g. the 4000 ha Caingorm Plateau) which would take too long to map in detail. In these instances more general surveys are deemed acceptable. Progress with biological surveys is well advanced over most of Britain. By April 1985 in England 85% of sites had been surveyed, with 80% or more in the North-West, West Midlands, East Midlands, East Anglian, South East and South Regions, with only the North East and South West regions lagging slightly behind with less than 80% of sites surveyed. In Wales, with fewer sites, progress is greater: 86% of sites had been surveyed. In Scotland the overall figure is 58%, with the North-West Region well ahead with 75% surveyed.

Two other tasks involving extensive legwork for the NCC's assistant regional officers (AROs) are the delimitation of the sssi boundary and the identification of all owners and occupiers. The boundary is often fairly straightforward to establish in the lowlands, although it requires quite detailed scientific survey on the ground, and time-consuming cartography. Again, the 'clean sweep' policy requires that all existing site boundaries are re-checked, and that where part of a site has been damaged it is removed, or, if necessary, additional valuable areas are incorporated. The boundary is particularly important because the implementation of the Act turns on the proper identification of owners and occupiers, with whom the NCC will have to deal over site management. This has proved a nightmare. Conventionally, SSSIs are portrayed as cosy little field corners owned by co-operative and communicative country gentlemen. That may be true in the Home Counties, but nowhere else. Sites can be extensive and can overlap onto several properties. Nationally, there is an average of five owners per site: in some cases far more. Registers of land in England are not sufficiently up to date to be useful, and usually the ARO has to resort to knocking on doors. Local landowners may not always be willing to give the information. Even if they are, many sites are complex because owned jointly, perhaps by brothers or a husband and wife, and there is the problem of people with temporary rights (e.g. of pasture) from the landowner. Legally *all* owners of any part of the SSSI have to be contacted, as does anyone with rights on any part of it. Common land is particularly difficult, since there may be literally hundreds of commoners who need to be notified. Areas such as the Lake District Fells or areas of saltmarsh are among those with large numbers of commoners. It is vastly time consuming to compile the register of owners and occupiers, not least because most AROs are ecologists not land experts, but it is a vital task on which the whole effectiveness of the Act rests: there have already been cases where owners have been prosecuted for damaging a renotified SSSI, and there has been legal debate on the validity of that notification if a single owner or occupier is left out.

Once all the data on the site are available, the NCC has to determine what operations are, in the words of the Act, 'likely to damage that flora or those features ... by reason of which the land is of special interest'. What the NCC has done is to produce a standardised list of what they call Potentially Damaging Operations (PDOs), and a cross tabulation showing which operations would normally be expected to be damaging in particular habitats. If for any reason the ARO believes one of these not to be relevant in any case, he has to say why, and this has to be duly approved. A full list of PDOs is given in the Appendix. Thus on a wet meadow, the changing of an existing grazing or mowing regime or the introduction of either, the application of manure, fertilizer, lime, pesticides (including weedkiller), dumping of materials and drainage would all be among the PDOs. In a woodland the cutting or removal of plant remains and changes in tree, woodland or game management would probably be most important, while on a coastal saltmarsh site the dumping or discharge of materials, change in fishing management, bait digging or sea defence work would be relevant. In many cases existing use of the site may include these uses, indeed in many important instances the scientific interest of the site will be closely dependent on the nature of existing human use. None the less, because of this interdependence of human use and wildlife interest, new activities or changes in the scale or intensity of use are likely to have implications for the structure or diversity of the plant and animal communities on the site. These activities are therefore classed as *potentially* damaging in order that their impact can be assessed.

The approval stage is important, both because the NCC itself is obviously desperately keen not to make any blunders in renotification, since it is an extremely sensitive issue, and also because the Act demands that the Council of the NCC itself is satisfied as to the value of each SSSI. What this means in practice is that the Chairman of the appropriate Country Advisory Committee sees the papers associated with each site and approves the renotification before the papers are served on each owner and occupier. Given the number of SSSIs to be renotified (over 4000 at the last count, 2000 of them in England) even this formality has proved a task of considerable magnitude. In England a total of 42% of sites had been approved by May 1985, the greatest proportion being in the North-East Region (61%), and the least in the West Midlands (30%).

The penultimate stages of renotification are the sending out of formal letters to owners and occupiers, the local planning authority, and the Secretary of State. This sounds easy, but in practice it has proved a legal quagmire, as attempted prosecutions for SSSI damage have revealed shortcomings in the procedure. These are discussed under 'enforcement' below. The last stage of all is the registration of the sssi as a land charge. This is fairly simple in England and Wales, but for various reasons is enormously complicated in Scotland. Everywhere it involves people skilled in land agency matters. Largely because the ncc is tied to low civil service salaries it finds land agents hard to recruit, and such expertise has been in crucially short supply since the Act was passed. Renotification has undoubtedly been slowed because of this. The negotiation of management agreements, which often begins as soon as a site is renotified, makes even heavier demands on the ncc's Land Agents, and the burden of work creates a significant and serious bottleneck in proceedings.

The procedure with the renotification of new sites is somewhat different, and has in fact already been amended (in 1985) to prevent damage to sssis during notification. In the original system, documents on each site were prepared in exactly the same way, but instead of notifying the site forthwith, a letter of intent was sent to owners and occupiers, the local planning authority and the Secretary of State. This gave full details about the proposed sssi, and was followed by a three month 'consultation period' within which, in the words of the Act, 'representations or objections can be made'. If no one objected, the site could be notified in due course. If any owner or occupier, or the local authority, objected, the ncc regional office had to prepare a summary of the scientific reasons for notification, and the substance of the objections, and the Country Advisory Committee chairman had to sit in judgement. He must consider any contrary scientific evidence and decide whether to reject objections and notify the site.

In practice, it was found that this procedure allowed an unsympathetic owner or occupier to carry out a pdo (kindly listed for him in the consultation letter) during the three month consultation period. In one case in Northamptonshire, for example, an owner bulldozed a grassland site to a depth of six inches in order not to be constrained in his building plans. The procedure was therefore altered to make this impossible as part of the Wildlife and Countryside (Amendment) Bill, passed – after many tribulations – in July 1985. This is discussed in more detail below.

It is important to be able to put the task of renotifying existing

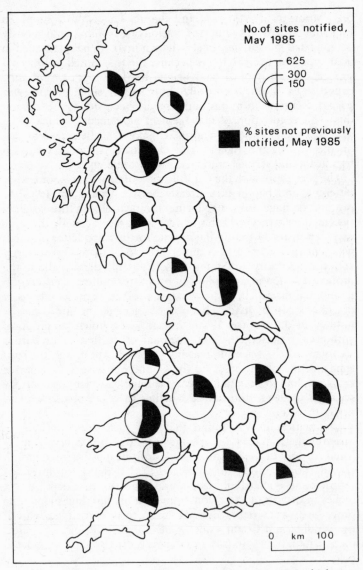

Figure 5.1 The proportion of sssis notified in May 1985 which were new to the sssi system, and not existing sites. The diagram also shows how many sites had been notified in each region.

SSSIs, and the notification of new sites into perspective. The total number of intended new sites, known as Proposed SSSIs, or PSSSIs, in May 1985 was 1848 in Britain as a whole, compared to 4051 existing sites. Thus 31% of the total list of SSSIs and PSSSIs are new sites. The figure is highest in Wales (40%) with as many as 55% of sites in Dyfed/Powys Region new, and lowest in England (28%) where only NE Region has over 40% (47%), while the East Midlands Region has only 19% of sites that are new (see Fig. 5.1). In Scotland the overall figure is 34%, with the greatest proportion of new sites in the South East Region (44%). The reason for these figures is partly that the Act has stimulated extensive extra survey efforts throughout Britain which have thrown up previously unknown sites. Other surveys, for example those of the Nature Conservation Trusts have also been fed into the system. Partly also, the Act has caused a great tightening-up of procedure and acceleration of work on the existing schedules. These were revised, or simply updated and added to, at intervals through the 1960s and 1970s, but often the work had got behind due to other pressing tasks. A substantial number of existing SSSIs have been damaged, or have lost their special interest for other reasons. These are being denotified by the NCC. The Act made the notification of all SSSI-quality sites paramount, and a great many sites already known about but not yet formally scheduled were added into the system as PSSSIs. In some counties the most recent schedule dates to the late 1970s (e.g. in England, Cheshire 1979, Hampshire in 1978, Cleveland, Dorset, Greater Manchester and Humberside 1977, some with subsequent partial revisions). In other cases the schedules were older, for example again in England, Bedfordshire (1971), Cambridgeshire (1971), Cornwall (1972) and Derbyshire as old as 1963. Given the growing focus on SSSIs at the end of the 1970s and during the passing and implementation of the Act, there were many important sites which had to be brought into the system.

Progress with the notification of new sites is a little slower than that of existing sites: in Britain as a whole, 52% of new sites identified by April 1985 had been surveyed, compared to 58% of existing sites; 38% of new sites had got to the consultation stage. Progress with new sites varied across the country, of course, with consultation begun in 48% of Scottish, 36% English and 33%

119

of Welsh psssis. The greatest variation in progress in individual regions was in England, for example 49% of psssis in North East Region having reached consultation compared to 15% of those in South East.

The cost of bureaucracy

Renotification obviously is not simple, nor should anyone have expected it to be done quickly. Slowly the number of sites notified and renotified has risen, and – equally slowly – the information revolution has started to transform the NCC's data handling. It has been a somewhat painful process, but there is now a standardised way of handling data about sssis called (with a creditable simulation of computer-talk) the Site Related Data Base, or SRDB, run on microcomputers. In the long term this will contain data about the site (location, name, etc.), scientific data (species lists, habitat areas), information on the tenure of the site and the PDOs listed, information on any legal matters relating to the site including all management agreements, records of all conservation management carried out, and a record of all 'casework', i.e. details of all applications to carry out PDOs and any damage which occurs.

This last category of information, the Casework Monitoring Scheme, will eventually allow complete statistics on sssi damage and loss to be compiled nationally or regionally, or in terms of the type of site or type and source of damage. When that is possible it will be invaluable to the NCC for planning its strategy, and indeed to everyone else (if the data are made available). The SRDB will eventually, perhaps 40 years after sssis were first created, provide the kind of hard data on damage and loss which has been conspicuously lacking so far. However, like the rest of the system, the Casework Monitoring Scheme is only just starting, and over-worked AROs are (understandably) reluctant to fill in the necessary forms to make the data available to the national headquarters' computer people. The data available to date is discussed in the context of sssi loss below.

None the less, the SRDB is getting under way. In Wales, with only some 860 sites in all, the data base itself is used as a record of progress with renotification. Scotland is moving the same way, but in England, with over 3600 sites, they have established a second register of the progress with renotification, and only put sites on the main data base once they are renotified or notified properly. Compatible statistics on a national level are, however, compiled from these various computer files, and they give a good picture of progress with renotification across the country.

The task varies. It is greatest in England (3657 sites), and least in Wales (864 sites). Regionally the number of sites varies also, with over 500 in four English regions, and less than 300 in two Welsh and one Scottish region (Fig. 5.2). Progress with renotification and notification tends to match the sheer number of sites. Progress is greatest in Wales (46% all sites by May 1985), followed by Scotland (36%) and lastly England (30%). None the less, there is considerable regional variation within this, the North West and East Midlands Region in England, Dyfed/Powys and South Region in Wales and North West and South East Region in Scotland being well on with over 40% of sites renotified (Fig. 5.2). The progress with renotification also varies at the regional scale, as Fig. 5.3 of the NCC's South Region, shows.

Obviously the renotification process is complicated, and hence slow, because of the limited number of regional staff in the NCC and the number of other jobs they have to do. Throughout the period of renotification there has been less than one ARO to each county, and of course some counties have more sites (and hence more work) than others. In 1983 the Rayner Review of the NCC calculated that renotification would require an additional 24 man-years of survey staff time on top of the existing 81 AROs in post. This suggestion that *more* staff were needed was a surprising conclusion from what was intended as a cost-cutting exercise, but the figure was still too low. Calculations by the NCC in England in 1983, based on experience up to that time, suggested that six man-days were required to notify each existing SSSI and nine for each PSSSI, allowing two farm visits. Using these figures, and the number of SSSIs identified in April 1985, the whole task was expected to involve 33 300 man-days of ARO time, or almost 140 man-years. With only about 80 AROs in post, there would be several years work if they could devote themselves to it full-time: but they cannot. All sorts of other jobs have to be done: dealing

121

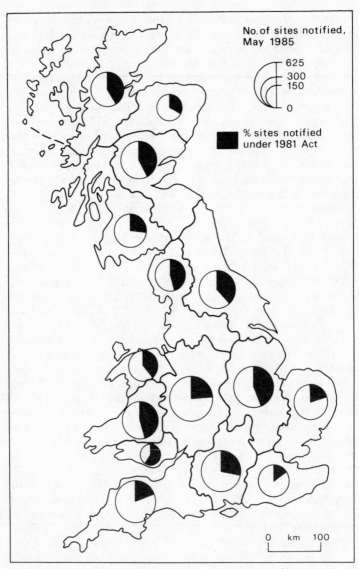

No. of sites notified, May 1985

625
300
150
0

■ % sites notified under 1981 Act

0   km   100

Figure 5.2 Progress with renotification: proportion of known sites in each region notified by May 1985 and the total number notified.

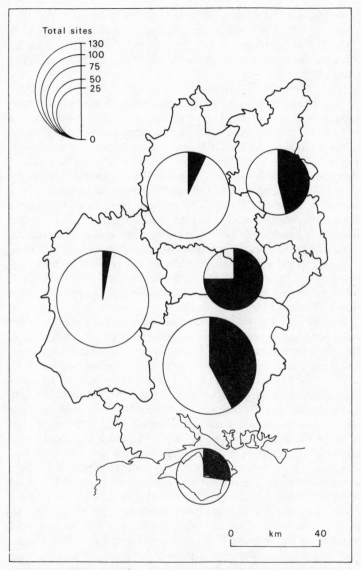

Figure 5.3 Progress with renotification: proportion of sites renotified by May 1985 in the NCC's South region.

with planning inquiries, requests for information about rare species, or bats in roofs, and advisory work of many kinds. In 1983 it was calculated that at most only 73% of an ARO's time could be devoted to renotification, and at that rate it would take until 1989 to finish.

It is quite clear that in work of this kind, progress is directly related to the number of staff employed, and hence how much money is put into it. The NCC has successfully sought and obtained increased income in the past three years. In 1983/4 the grant-in-aid was £11.69 million, a small increase on previous years. In 1984/5 it was increased by 36% to £18.1 million, and in the year 1985/6 the NCC's Corporate Plan (pushed through by the NCC's new chairman, William Wilkinson, a banker) won a further increase of 25% to £22.7 million. The 1986/7 budget has been substantially increased again to £32.1 million. The allocation of money specifically to renotification has also increased, from £220 000 1983/4, to £660 000 in the current year 1985/86. The rate of progress with renotification has risen in response, from only 5 sites per month between August 1982 and March 1983 to 36 per month 1983/84, and 50 per month in the last financial year 1984/5.

In renotification, you get what you pay for. New regional staff have been appointed to assist with the paperwork on each site, but there is no magic wand to guarantee instant completion. There are still bottlenecks in the system, both of decision making at the regional staff level, and most particularly in the shortage of land agents. In May 1985 the then Parliamentary Under Secretary of State, William Waldegrave, announced to the Commons that the NCC had confirmed that it could bring forward the completion of sssi renotification 'from 1987 to 1986, which is a satisfactory outcome in response to the additional money which it has received'. This promise is extremely unlikely to be fulfilled. There are a number of figures for the likely date of completion of renotification in circulation. Some are what are known as 'management targets', i.e. they are dates which AROs are being asked to aim for, and some are calculated on the basis of computer returns of progress so far. Neither is an entirely sure guide, because no two sites are the same. Some present far more difficulties than others, and who is to know if the ARO has done the easy ones first to get them out of the way (and create an impression of industry), or done the most complicated or sensitive first? Rates of progress vary considerably between regions: in England in the year ending March 1985, South-East Region renotified an average of only 2.9 sites per month, while the North-East, East Midlands and West Midlands did over seven. To a large extent this is due to a number of complex cases developing over renotifications in the South-East which absorbed vast amounts of the ARO's time.

Until sites are duly notified, none of the powers of the Act can be applied to them. Obviously it is vital to complete the re-notification process quickly, and equally obviously delay is embarrassing to the NCC. So too, however, will be fake pre-dictions. It is likely that 80% of existing SSSIs will be renotified in Wales by the end of 1986, slightly less likely that those in Scotland will be done by the same time. Eighty percent com-pletion in England will probably take until 1988. The notification of new sites will take longer, and it is likely that there will be a long tail of sites not properly notified well on into the next decade. To all intents and purposes, renotification as a task may last indefinitely, gradually evolving into a rolling programme of revision. Until it is completed, or virtually completed, SSSIs and PSSSIs will be particularly vulnerable because they are unpro-tected by the Act.

There are several quite specific dangers arising from the bureaucratic quagmire of renotification. First, it has increasingly become an obsession, both within and outside the NCC. The AROs have little time for anything other than preparing the vast bundle of papers associated with each site: other duties, especially the need to be involved in decision making in the wider countryside, have inevitably suffered. The Act, and its focus on SSSIs, has delivered the final *coup de grâce* to an integrated role for the NCC, narrowing its focus to the SSSI system, and tying up its regional staff in a web of bureaucracy. The implications for the wider countryside have yet to be fully realised. This is related to the second danger: renotification has been such a problem within the NCC, and has attracted such attention from commentators and critics outside, that there is a very real danger that it will become an end in itself. What was conceived in the heat of Parliamentary debate as a constructive way of making sure that everyone knew

125

exactly why each sssi was important has flowered into a massive, legalistic and bureaucratic procedure. But renotification does not protect sssis – it was never intended to. All it does is open the way to an early warning system about damage, and a mechanism for concluding management agreements. Although it seems an impossible enough task, renotification is really only the beginning of site protection. There is a danger that this is being forgotten. Renotification is easy compared to the problems of the casework arising from it.

Casework

Renotification is but the curtain-raiser to the business of protecting the sssi system. Once renotified or newly notified, any owner or occupier wanting to carry out a potentially damaging operation has to give the NCC due notice, in writing. The NCC then may respond by giving consent or, (as would frequently be the case) they may refuse to give permission to proceed. The whole procedure of offering a management agreement then begins. This all seems very straightforward, but there are manifold problems.

Foremost among them is simply the fact that every site which is renotified is liable to generate further work in the form of either the need to explain what is involved to the owner or occupier, or to start talking about agreements, or both. This 'casework', as it is known, therefore tends to increase as the work of notification proceeds. Every step towards the completion of renotification involves several steps sideways to handle the casework arising. This is no imaginary problem: in June 1984 a total of 230 000 ha had been renotified in Britain, and management agreements had been sought on 63 000 ha (28%). The percentage was much lower in Wales (12%), about the GB level in Scotland (25%), but high in England, where management agreements had been sought over almost 30 000 ha, 48% of the area renotified. The NCC is currently working on the assumption that one third of sssis will need agreements eventually.

This casework mountain is, of course, one of the chief reasons why renotification is taking so long: however unimportant it is, once a site is threatened by a PDO, it has to take top priority or else it is likely to be damaged or lost. Negotiations over PDOs and management agreements move to their own tight timetable, which cannot be ignored without putting sites at risk.

To an extent the amount of casework which follows renotification depends on the way that it is done. One strategy is to devote time to explaining the nature and importance of the SSSI to the owner or occupier and thus hope to soften the blow of the bundle of uninterpretable paperwork which will presently thud through their letterbox. The idea here is to avoid any sense of alienation and frustration which might lead to precipitate damage. This approach has been widely adopted in England, and obviously the 'farm gate' discussion is very much in the spirit of the NCC's traditional approach of co-operation and consensus. The trouble is that even if it avoids ill-will, once the restriction associated with holding an SSSI, and the possibility of a rather generous management agreement, are explained, many owners and occupiers want to go ahead and sort everything out by obtaining one forthwith. There may be less danger of losing the site by this approach, but in the long run it makes for just as much casework. Also, the early discussions mean that renotification is likely to be slower, which as we have seen is far from satisfactory.

The alternative strategy is to treat the renotification as a purely formal process. The papers are prepared and sent out without much prior discussion, and the ARO hopes to be able to handle any backlash from those alienated by the sudden rush of bureaucracy. This approach has been adopted widely in Wales, and a number of English regions seem to be moving towards it. In Wales it allowed faster initial progress with renotification, but of course it does make it more likely that owners and occupiers will be resentful and hence unco-operative, which makes the eventual casework doubly time-consuming and difficult to handle. It is six of one and half-a-dozen of the other: there is no ideal strategy. From the ARO's point of view, both approaches have significant drawbacks.

Much of the legwork involved in discussion with owners and occupiers falls on the ARO, but once the basic principle of the kind of management required are understood the burden passes to the NCC's lands office. The difficulties with setting out management agreements are described in the next chapter, but the sheer financial complexity plus the novelty of the work for all surveyors (the NCC's own tiny staff, private advisors and the district valuers), creates enormous delays. Although some are simple, some agreements are taking up to two years to conclude. The NCC is looking towards perhaps 10 000 agreements over the next 10 years. Less than 1000 have been concluded so far: the mountain of casework has clearly barely begun to be climbed.

The fact that agreements can take two years to process highlights the unrealistic nature of the Act's provisions. Internally they are consistent, but they match badly with the real world. Section 28 of the Act was modified by an Amendment Act in 1985 to allow four months (not three) for the conclusion of management agreements. Even so, this is too short in most cases. What happens is that an interim agreement is entered into for perhaps a further three months while negotiations continue, and this is renewed until the full agreement (backdated of course) is concluded, or the whole system breaks down. This arrangement works, after a fashion, but is cumbersome (it means even more paperwork), and unsatisfactory for both parties. This is just one of several ways in which the Act is being implemented by rather ramshackle and *ad hoc* arrangements. It misses being altogether unworkable by a narrow margin.

Arrangements under the Act are unsatisfactory in other ways also. Farmers tend by nature to be conservative, and to have a healthy (and quite commendable) dislike of unfavourable bureaucracy, and yet the Act is the epitomy of the 'red tapeworm'. Many of the problems the NCC has experienced in getting the measure of the new legislation stem from their reluctance to see how difficult it is to blend their old back-of-envelope and farm-gate approach to site protection with the legalistic and administrative tightness of the Act. Farmers are no more pleased by this onset of officialdom. Quite apart from the unpalatable nature of the procedure, it is far from well suited to the real world. If the PDOs include 'changing the intensity of grazing', then the NCC really needs a letter from a farmer saying 'I was grazing this area 5 cows per hectare, I now wish to double this'. To this they can respond in the required fashion. They are much more likely to get a telephone call, probably some time after the event, and in most cases are unlikely to know what is happening at all. Most farmers do not make decisions with flowcharts and written plans (whatever MAFF might like), and if the truth be told, neither by inclination do most conservationists. The Act, however, requires just this kind of compartmentalised and bureaucratised thinking. This is another reason why its implementation has been difficult.

Closing loopholes

Criticisms of the Wildlife and Countryside Act have tended to focus not on the general problems of implementation, but specific shortcomings in the provision of Sections 28 and 29. These 'loopholes', as they became known, made it possible for the intentions of the Act to be eroded and SSSIs destroyed. As their existence became clear, so did pressure to amend the Act to close the loopholes. They were finally closed, although not to universal satisfaction, in the summer of 1985 when the Wildlife and Countryside (Amendment) Act was finally passed by Parliament.

The most blatant loophole was that in Section 28(2). The 1981 Act allowed for a three-month consultation period before any new site (PSSSI), or an extension to an existing site, could be officially notified. During that period its only protection lay in the good nature of the owner or occupier, who was under no legal obligation to refrain from carrying out damaging operations or to tell the NCC if he did. While the NCC and CLA urged their members to do nothing to damage a PSSSI in this period (above all to do nothing to rock the boat with regard to the voluntary principle), not all owners and occupiers were well-disposed. Thus, in July 1982, 10 ha of a lowland valley mire and grassland site in Dyfed in Wales, Rhos Derlwyn-Fawr, were ploughed during consultation over notification, damaging the interest of the site to the extent that it was no longer worthy of notification. Early in 1983, immediately prior to notification by the NCC, some 3 ha of a limestone grassland site at Kingsthorpe Scrub Field in Northants were bulldozed by the owner. Another example of difficulties caused by the enforced three-month delay in notification is that of Lashford Home Fen in Oxfordshire, which was raised in the

Commons in February 1985 by Tony Baldry MP when the Amendment Bill was being read for the second time. The NCC was in the process of notifying the 7 ha site, which was owned by the Thames Water Authority. The Berkshire, Buckinghamshire and Oxfordshire Naturalists Trust was negotiating to buy 6 ha of the site for £15 000, but a property speculator had offered £25 000 for the remaining 1 ha block, and had advertised its availability for housing plots (without planning permission) in 12 plots at £5000 each. The survival of the site promised to be a race between the slow process of renotification (which would at least have allowed the NCC the right to a say in the future of the site) and the other negotiations. In the event, the DOE leaned on the Thames Water Authority and cited their statutory duty to further nature conservation under the 1981 Act and the speculator withdrew. As Tony Baldry MP commented 'if the SSSI notification had been immediate, none of this need have happened'.

It would be possible to go on enumerating examples of site damage because of the 'Section 28 loophole', but these will suffice. By 1983, two years after the Act was passed, it had become clear that SSSIs and PSSSIs were continuing to be lost and damaged. In November, Wildlife Link published statistics on loss in their second Habitat Report. The NCC's Tenth Annual Report, for the year ending March 1984, confirmed observers' impressions: 156 SSSIs had been damaged in the year and damage to a further 20 sites has appeared subsequently. In their turn, FOE published a report *SSSIs 1984: failure of the Wildlife and Countryside Act* which enumerated damaged sites, and pointed the finger at, among other problems, the Section 28 loophole. NCC data show that by October 1984 there had been at least 328 cases of damage to sites in England alone, of which 19% concerned PSSSIs. Of these 62 cases, 23% involved damage during the period of consultation, the 'loophole' in protection. Of course most of the rest – i.e. the majority of damage – concerned existing SSSIs not yet renotified.

The question of loopholes in the Act was raised with the Secretary of State by various individuals and organisations (including the NCC) in May 1984, but the first attempt to close the Section 28 loophole was by Peter Hardy MP in a Private Members Bill in July 1984. The wording of the Act is complicated, and there were certain drafting problems with his Bill, but the real problem was that it was sat on by the government. They gave assurances that they would introduce legislation in government time to deal with the loophole and other matters, although they failed to do so. The matter eventually came before Parliament again in February 1985 when (by pure chance) the ballot of Private Members Bills fell to another MP interested in conservation, the opposition spokesman on the environment David Clark, and in the second Reading debate he stressed how the government had twice in 1984 failed to take up the Opposition's offer of co-operation in amending the Act. Another member said he was 'deeply disappointed' that the government had not come forward with their own legislation to close the loopholes.

In the meantime, the 'loopholes' question had been taken up again in the work of the House of Commons Select Committee on the Environment which took evidence on the Act in November. In their evidence, the NCC reported the destruction of two sites and serious damage to 12 others during the consultation period. These included an area of grassland and marsh at Ripon Parks in Yorkshire which was rotivated and treated with pesticides in May 1982 following consultation, and a hay meadow in Northamptonshire, Gillets Meadow, which was destroyed by ploughing in February 1984. Concern at the existence of the 'three month loophole' was shared by almost all those who gave evidence to the Select Committee, including the NFU and CLA who saw the danger of unworkable legislation. In their report in February 1985, the Committee urged its closure.

They also gave attention to a second loophole, in Section 29 of the Act. This provides for an NCO imposed by the Secretary of State, and its use can be recommended by the NCC where it has been unable to negotiate a management agreement or outright purchase within the three-month period allowed. As we have seen, most management agreements (even with amenable owners) take more than three months to negotiate. If negotiations broke down, very rapid action was required to prevent site damage, and the procedure for obtaining a Section 29 order was not fast. The NCC had to submit a detailed formal case to the secretary of state, who then consulted other government departments (including MAFF). This could take some weeks: so if the

131

order was to be ready at the end of the three-month period it had to be applied for well ahead. This added to the already excessive work of concluding the agreement, implied a lack of trust in the intentions of the owner or occupier, and ran the risk that the Secretary of State would refuse to make the NCO because the voluntary approach had not been exhausted.

The House of Commons Select Committee argued that 'all parties are agreed that these loopholes need to be closed'. Their report appeared on 16 January 1985, and on 8 February their statement was put to the test when David Clark's Wildlife and Countryside (Amendment) Bill was debated in the Commons. It contained six clauses, one of which (Clause 2) related to Section 28 of the 1981 Act. The rest concerned stronger measures on badger digging (Clause 1), greater powers for the NCC to declare Marine Nature Reserves (Clause 3), new requirements on both the Ministry of Agriculture and the FC to further nature conservation (Clauses 4 and 6) and an extension of the moorland maps in national parks (Clause 5). As it turned out, the sharpest debate was focused on these other clauses, particularly that concerning the Ministry of Agriculture (which was thrown out in the Committee stage in March) and those on marine nature reserves and the FC (both of which were emasculated in Committee). Over Clause 2 there was embarrassingly little dispute.

In introducing the Bill, David Clark stressed 'we are discussing a concensus Bill – that cannot be said too firmly', and also pointed out the strength of public opinion: 'there is a tide of opinion so great that the Bill is the minimum that people will accept'.

Clause 2 was the fruit of a long period of careful drafting and close liaison with the DOE. It was, Clark said 'a very complicated matter. In the end he had to use diagrams'. Complicated or not, the House took it on board: Sir John Farr MP commented 'the sooner we can get on to the statute book the amendment set out in Clause 2, the better'; Nicholas Lyell MP said 'I believe that all hon. Members agree that it is high time we closed the three-months' loophole', and Kenneth Carlisle MP, author of *Conserving the countryside: a Tory view*, said 'Clause 2, which must be passed, will stop the ignorant or malicious destruction of our best sites, which has occurred since 1981'.

What Clause 2 did was to bring forward the date of official notification to the beginning, not the end, of the period of consultation. This meant that a new site was formally covered by the Act from the moment the letter containing details was sent to the owner or occupier: at no time thereafter could he carry out a damaging operation without notifying the NCC in the usual way. He still had three months in which to object to the notification, and anyway the NCC would have to either confirm the notification (possibly with modifications reducing the area or specified operations) or withdraw it within nine months. If it were not confirmed, the notification would lapse. This sounds simple, but the Bill is a masterpiece of complex drafting.

The Bill promised to close the three month loophole, but was less effective in providing an improved procedure for Section 29 orders. Sir Hugh Rossi MP, chairman of the Select Committee, said in the Commons 'I regret that the Bill does not follow the Select Committee's recommendation about closing the loopholes in Section 29 of the Act'. He felt that 'the hon. Gentleman has allowed the Department (of the Environment) to distract his attention from imposing a completely watertight closure of the loophole'. What the Bill did was to extend the period for negotiation of a management agreement (and during which the notified operations could not be carried out) from three months to four months. This would supposedly allow the NCC an extra month to obtain a Section 29 order from the secretary of state. It also allowed for an agreement to extend this period, with a month to elapse between any breakdown of negotiations and the owner or occupier's freedom to develop the site, during which time a Section 29 Order could be sought. The NCC themselves, in their evidence to the Select Committee, called for the power to make a 'Stop Order' on their own decision to prevent all work for a period of one month. This the Select Committee endorsed. Sir Hugh Rossi pointed out that although the provision of the Bill 'affords a modest amount of protection' it fell short of this aim. However, at the Committee stage it was confirmed that 'it is certainly the view of the NCC that it has time to bring forward a Nature Conservation Order under this provision if things go wrong'.

Although many other aspects of the Bill were changed at the

Commons Committee, the clauses designed to close the loopholes survived. The Bill went before the Committee on 6 March, was debated at the Report Stage in the Commons on 26 April and went to the Lords. It received its first reading on 30 April, was read for a second time and debated on 17 May and was debated in a Committee of the whole House on 12 June. It completed its third reading in June and went back to the Commons where it passed in early July. It came into force on 26 August. Finally the loopholes had been closed. Despite the length and intensity of debate and political manoevering, the vast bulk of the provisions of the 1981 Act were unchanged. Many problems remain.

Stopping site loss

The Wildlife and Countryside Act lays great stress on the positive aspect of site protection, though management agreements concluded voluntarily between the NCC and the owners or occupiers of sssis. The danger of slow renotification and the practical and political difficulties with the procedure set down have been described above. The enormous financial problems are described below. These comprise the 'carrot' aspect of site protection. There are also provisions for the application of the stick to keep unwilling owners or occupiers within certain bounds. There are severe limitations with these.

The NCO is the most available extra protection for an sssi where normal negotiations over management have broken down. One problem with it is the delay between the NCC asking for an order and the secretary of state granting it. This 'loophole', and the attempts to close it, have already been described. More fundamental, and more dangerous, is a difference in opinion between the NCC and the DOE as to whether an order can be made on any sssi. The Act itself allows an order to be made on land which *in the opinion of the Secretary of State* is of 'special interest', and of 'national importance'. The common interpretation of this by the NCC and the voluntary bodies is that all sssis are of special interest (quite literally by definition: if they were not special they would not be notified) and the whole sssi system is a network of national importance. This has been the NCC's view since it revised its SSSI selection guidelines in 1979. No site will be renotified under the 1981 Act unless it is of national importance. The DOE, however, maintains that the case for the special importance of each SSSI has to be made each time, and if it is inadequate the Secretary of State will not grant an NCO. Furthermore, in the original debates about the Bill in 1981 various figures of the number of sites where the Section 29 order might be used were mentioned. Lord Avon spoke of 'about half a dozen' and 'can be any number' on 12 February 1981. Tom King mentioned '40 to 50 initially' in the Commons on 4 June while Earl Ferrers made it clear on 12 March that only cost might prevent orders being made on all SSSIS. Subsequently the Secretary of State decided that the Parliamentary debates did not support the notion that all SSSIS are of national interest, but this is not borne out by *Hansard*. No figure such as 40 'super' SSSIS has any statutory basis, but has stuck, and become part of the mass of erroneous folk wisdom about the Act. In his handbook on the Act for chartered surveyors, Barry Denyer-Green writes 'Nature Conservation Orders are intended for those areas of exceptional interest, nationally and sometimes internationally. It has been suggested that up to forty such areas may initially be involved'. This issue is still not finally resolved.

In August 1982 the NCC wrote a policy statement on the Act which confirmed their intention to use all its powers to protect all SSSIS. They have maintained this position, in public at least. A conflict has therefore developed between their desire to be able to call for a Section 29 order on any SSSI, and the Secretary of State's desire to be convinced that every site is of national importance. As might be imagined, the idea of 'key sites', especially those in the Nature Conservation Review, has become mixed up in this. Some (even in the NCC) see the Section 29 order as an appropriate defence for Nature Conservation Review sites but not 'ordinary' SSSIS, arguing that if the secretary of state is determined to restrict their number then it is wisest to be sure the best sites are most firmly protected. Others argue that there was never any scientific basis for grading sites, which form a continuum of quality, and that it is both a breach of principle and a dangerous precedent to do other than push for Section 29 orders on all SSSIS.

The question seemed to be answered in 1983 when there was a

135

Public Inquiry into the NCO on Baddesley Common SSSI in Hampshire. The SSSI comprises an area of bog, grassland and heath, and was scheduled in 1979. It was not included in the Nature Conservation Review. Resurvey following the passage of the 1981 Act showed that part of the area had been damaged by agricultural activities, and a greatly reduced area (15 ha) was renotified under the Act in July 1982. A few days later formal notice was received from the owners of part of the site, who wished to clear, drain and plough the area. The NCC objected, declined an offer to buy part of the area affected, and offered a management agreement. This was refused, and since the owner intended to go ahead with the development of the site at the end of the three month period, the NCC sought an NCO which was granted in October 1982. The owner appealed, and a public inquiry was held in March 1983. In July 1983, on the advice of the inspector the Secretary of State upheld the order.

This case shows the limitation of the Section 29 order, the time taken to set up the public inquiry had used up the negotiation period allowed following the giving of notice and the site was still not protected. To extend the period of protection, the NCC had to commence compulsory purchase procedures, although in the end they bought it without resort to a compulsory purchase order (CPO). None the less, it seemed to demonstrate that an 'ordinary' SSSI could be protected by a Section 29 order, and the case was widely interpreted as such by the conservation movement. Subsequent events have made the situation less clear. In March 1985 Patrick Jenkin told the Commons in a written answer to a Parliamentary question that 14 NCOs had been made, 10 in England and two each in Scotland and Wales. A further three had been refused. He said 'I was not fully satisfied that the sites met the criteria set out in Section 29 of the Act'. Those refused included Brimham Rocks SSSI and Sherburn Willows PSSSI, both in North Yorkshire. The former was threatened by a pig farm, the latter by the excavation of ponds. Both were small sites (just over 2 ha). The applications were made late in 1984, and in both cases were rejected on the grounds that the sites were not of national importance. The location of the sites where NCOs have been sought are shown in Figure 5.4.

The implication of these remarkable decisions have yet to be

136

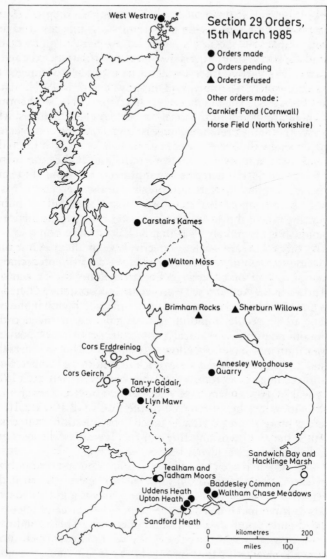

Figure 5.4 Location of sites where Section 29 Orders had been applied for by 15 March 1985.

worked out, but if the DOE persist in taking on themselves the judgement of the relative importance of SSSIs, this could have a serious impact on the NCC's ability to use the Act's powers to defend the SSSI system. This is the more important since the NCC's only recourse beyond a Section 29 order is to seek to acquire the site compulsorily. They have had this power since 1949, but it has rarely been used. The NCC has never liked to seem heavy-handed, and there are manifold practical and economic difficulties. The most serious in the present instance is simply that the CPO *also* has to be signed by the Secretary of State. If he has refused an NCO, he is unlikely to approve compulsory purchase. If the NCO is not approved, the SSSI is therefore left unprotected. It would not have been sought if the site were not threatened: the Secretary of State therefore can ignore his statutory conservation advisers and decide the fate of the most threatened sites on other, unspecified, grounds. It is alarmingly clear that he has taken to doing so.

The other key area where effectiveness of the 1981 Act in achieving its own aims is unclear is in the area of enforcement. When an owner or occupier deliberately flouts the procedures laid down in the Act, can he be prosecuted successfully? There are two questions here. The first is whether the NCC regional office is willing to prosecute, mindful as they must be of the need to maintain relations with local people. In some cases possible prosecution may have been allowed to slip away, but in others the owner has so clearly been a maverick that nothing has been lost by proceeding. In certain cases this has even had tacit NFU approval where farmers have rejected their advice. Increasingly such matters are being referred to the NCC's GB headquarters, where a more strategic view is taken. The question then arises whether the NCC, working through the Treasury Solicitor, can win their case. The evidence here is depressing.

Three cases had been heard by July 1985. The first resulted in a conviction, the latter two did not. The first case concerned the Ulverscroft Valley SSSI in Leicestershire. This is a grassland site, and the farmer had limed it. In September 1984 he came to court, pleaded guilty, and was fined £200 plus costs. The second case concerned a farmer in Dyfed in Wales who ploughed half of an 8 ha watermeadow site, Gwynnydd Yr Afon Fach, without notifying the NCC. He was tried in March 1985 and escaped on a technicality: the letter sent out by the NCC to all owners of PSSSIS invited comments, but did not make explicit that they had a right to object to the notification. The third case, where a farmer in Hertfordshire had ploughed part of Broadstone Meadow SSSI to plant swedes, went the same way in April 1985. The farmer retained a QC who established to the court's satisfaction that the NCC could not *prove* that the owner had received the notification letter. The Act itself did not specify how notification should be made. The two cases also raised a number of other alarming points. If land was held by joint owners, did both have to be notified? If a single owner on an SSSI was not notified, did this invalidate the whole notification? Did the NCC also have to prove that the local planning authority and the Secretary of State had actually received notification of the site?

Two sites had been damaged, and the NCC had no recourse. More seriously, deep legal flaws were revealed in the minutiae of the renotification process. The NCC put a moritorium on all new notifications for a month, and took legal advice. Morale among regional staff hit rock bottom. The NCC was advised that there was little point in appealing against these particular decisions, but there seemed no watertight way of serving the notification papers without demanding that the AROs become glorified bailiffs, and deliver them in person with a witness. Eventually a brief new Bill was rushed through Parliament and the Wildlife and Countryside (Service of Notices) Act 1985 passed. This quite simply tied the procedure for notification to that long established in the field of town planning by reference to the Town and Country Planning Act 1971 and the equivalent Scottish Act of 1972. Sanity returned, and the notification of new sites began again. Had the debate of the 1981 Act been less hectic, and the Bill better drafted in the first place, this trouble could have been avoided. In the meantime, some 500 new sites have been notified under the old, flawed, system. It remains to be seen in how many of these cases the notification is challenged in a court of law: the NCC is monitoring the situation closely, crossing its fingers and hoping. It plans a five-year technical review of the Act in 1986 which should highlight areas needing amendment.

These problems aside, it is clear that the Act has not by any means stopped the loss and damage of SSSIs. By the end of April

The SSSI system

Total No. of sites damaged
1983-84 156
1984-85 255

Figure 5.5   The proportion of SSSIs damaged, April 1983 – March 1984 (other categories include motorcycle scrambling, tipping, construction works, and quarrying).

1985 the revision of the total number of SSSIs in England involved a net loss of 105 old SSSIs. In Wales the loss was two, in Scotland a considerable gain in aggregate of 103 sites. This is seen more clearly in the figure for denotified sites – those which have had to be formally removed from the register because their interest has been destroyed. By April 1984 a total of 46 sites had been denotified in Great Britain. The figure for proposed denotifications, however, is far larger and far more alarming. In England at the end of May 1985 a total of 266 SSSIs were expected to be denotified, 10% of the existing SSSIs. The proportion rose as high as 13% in the West Midlands region, 14% in the South, 15% in the East Midlands and 19% in East Anglia. Some of these are geological sites replaced by superior examples in the course of the long-running Geological Conservation Review, but a substantial number are biological sites, and reflect damage or deterioration.

These are alarming figures, but the number of sites damaged is even greater. The NCC's Tenth Report gave figures for site damage in the year ending March 1984: 156 SSSIs and PSSSIs had been damaged, 43% seriously (Fig. 5.5). The Eleventh Report showed that damage increased in the next year: 255 sites were damaged in the year ending March 1985, 37% sustaining long-term or

140

permanent damage. On one third of sites the damage was serious enough that it could cause partial renotification, and 8 sites were so damaged as to warrant denotification of the whole site. In 54% of cases damage was expected to be long term. The data starting to appear from the new site related date base casework monitoring scheme are also depressing. By 30 June 1985 1228 report forms had been received. This represents but the tip of the iceberg, many counties being slow to adopt the new data recording methods. Of these cases, 333 (32%) involved notification of damaging operations, and 147 (14%) planning applications. Others involved less potentially destructive enquiries, including those from voluntary conservation bodies.

To an extent this activity shows the Act works, in as much as it provides a trigger mechanism for discussing the future of SSSIs. Equally, while most damaged sites are those not yet notified, 52% in 1984–85, some sites which enter one end of that tunnel of discussion are coming out at the other end damaged in some way. The factor which determines whether the site is conserved or destroyed is whether the owner or occupier is prepared to accept a management agreement. These agreements, and their staggering financial implications, are described in the next chapter.

Further reading

Adams, W. M. 1984. *Implementing the Act: a study of habitat protection under Part II of the Wildlife and Countryside Act 1981*. Oxford: British Association of Nature Conservationists and World Wildlife Fund.

Adams, W. M. 1984. Sites of Special Scientific Interest and habitat protection: implications of the Wildlife and Countryside Act 1981. *Area* 16(4), 273–80.

Barton, P. M. and G. P. Buckley, 1983. The status and protection of notified SSSIs in South-East England. *Biological Conservation* 27, 213–42.

Denyer-Green, B. 1983. *The Wildlife and Countryside Act 1981: the practitioner's companion*. London: Surveyors Publications.

Marren, P. 1983. A dog's life? *ECOS* 4(4), 34–46.

Nature Conservancy Council 1981–5. *Annual Reports*, Nos. 8–11.

Nature Conservancy Council, 1984. *Nature conservation in Great Britain*. Peterborough: Nature Conservancy Council.

141

Chapter Six

Conservation, money and the land

The Financial Guidelines

It took 15 months after the Wildlife and Countryside Act was passed to produce the final version of the *Financial Guidelines for management agreements*. They were finally published on 31 January 1983, as a joint circular from the DOE, MAFF and the Welsh Office, and came into effect at the end of February. Although it was claimed that the Guidelines had 'been prepared in consultation with a wide range of interested parties', the NCC had played almost no part in their preparation, although farming organisations had been consulted extensively. It is not surprising in the light of this to find that the Guidelines followed those developed in Exmoor and were designed primarily to maintain the owner or occupier's income.

Section 32 of the Act requires the NCC to offer a management agreement to an owner or occupier when they object to an application for a farm capital grant under the Agriculture Act 1970, and the Agriculture Minister refuses it. Procedures for applying for such grants were changed in 1980 (with the intention of saving MAFF money) and they were applied for retrospectively, after the work had been done. The 1981 Act restored the previous system on SSSIs (and in National Parks), so the NCC gets advance warning of application for grants for operations which could damage SSSIs. Under the Act, if the NCC's objection

142

to a grant caused it to be refused they are legally bound to offer a management agreement within three months. The farmer does not have to accept, of course, and there are provisions in the Guidelines for short term agreements of six months or a year (at a 'nominal sum', although some have not been) while they argue about it, and also for arbitration.

The Guidelines offer farmers a choice of a lump sum payment of an amount 'equal to the difference between the restricted and unrestricted value of the owner or owner–occupier's interest', or an annual payment which 'should reflect net profits foregone because of the agreement'. Both kinds of agreement might run for 20 years, or some other agreed period. Tenants can only receive annual payments, but the Guidelines point out that agreements would not run between tenancies so it is important to bring landlords in, again hopefully by 'a nominal payment'. Of the two, the annual payment is in general very much more favourable to the farmer, particularly as the Guidelines call for adjustments every year 'to reflect annual changes in farm productivity and profitability'. This effectively index-links the annual payments, within the limits of farm profitability.

Payments under the Guidelines are made on the assumption that 'but for the conservation considerations, farm capital grant *would* have been payable'. That also pushes the cost up, although the farmer's capacity to actually carry out the proposed work, and the ceiling on grants, have to be taken into account. The NCC only escapes paying for the grant element if the proposed operation is ineligible, the business is not in fact an agricultural business, or the operation is begun before the Agriculture Minister actually refuses the grant application (which of course he may not do if he thinks the SSSI unworthy, or the possible damage insignificant). There is no consideration of whether the operation is in fact desirable (from any point of view except that of the thwarted farmer), or sensible, only whether it is eligible for grant. The NCC thus ends up paying conservation money in place of MAFF money intended to increase production. The Guidelines therefore reduce MAFF expenditure at the expense of the NCCs, a fact which has infuriated conservationists since the rules were introduced. Payments also include the subsidy element in the price of farm production, a problem discussed further below. To cap it all, the NCC has to pay the costs of the farmer's professional advisers.

The Guidelines were greeted with hostility by conservation commentators, Malcolm MacEwan's comment on annual payments was typically succinct: 'management agreements on these terms can be likened to hot air balloons which can only be kept afloat by burning money'. One problem, realised some time before they were published, was that the Act covered only one of the kinds of grants available to British farmers. The NCC considered that the principle of compensation could not be applied to some owners and occupiers and not others without risking site losses because of uncertainty, so they voluntarily agreed to treat all other farm capital grants (including the Crofting Counties Agricultural Grants Scheme) in exactly the same way, and ('normally', whatever that means) grants or felling permission under forestry legislation. An annex to the Guidelines covers forestry operations, although, of course, these were never debated in Parliament, and are not mentioned in the Act. These allow for lump sum payments based on a comparison of discounted streams of expenditure and income over a given period (i.e. expected income and costs adjusted for inflation and interest rates) or a sum based on the depreciation in value of the land. The landowner could also opt for annual payments derived from the lump sum and adjusted to take account of current interest rates. These proposals make for a particularly intricate financial nightmare, which makes the quite considerable problems of working out agricultural payments fade into relative insignificance. They are also unrealistic, because the financial attractions of private forestry are far more dependent on potential tax benefits than any value of the timber. These problems are discussed further below.

The Guidelines may seem straightforward, but there have been very considerable practical problems with their application in the real world. The NCC had relatively little need of qualified land agents prior to the Act, and has had a lot of difficulty in building up its strength in this area. In the summer of 1985 they were seeking 10 extra land agents, and were having difficulties attracting them because of low salaries and the unusual (and limited) nature of the work. They are likely to need to go on using outside assistance for some time to come. However, staff shortages are only part of the problem. The Guidelines in fact present daunting technical problems of valuation. They demand detailed prediction of yields, variable costs (e.g. seed, fertilisers, pesticides, feedstuffs) and fixed costs (machinery, mortgage repayments, capital works like roads) which are beyond the normal range of experience of valuers. Great dependence is placed on District Valuers, but they have had to learn the new work, and indeed special courses have been devised to give training in the calculation of payments under the Guidelines. Interestingly, the District Valuers pushed for lump-sum payments while the form of the Guidelines was first being discussed. This would have been much simpler, and indeed much cheaper for the NCC, but they were overruled.

Two particular aspects of the Guidelines have been criticised extensively by conservationists. Both are complicated, and both have been highlighted by one man, John Bowers, an economist from the University of Leeds. John Bowers became the champion of conservation by taking the offensive against the Ministry of Agriculture in the field of economics, which is very much a closed book to most conservationists. As a result, his name is reviled by MAFF to almost the same extent as it is revered by those in conservation. He has done battle particularly over the economic evaluation of land drainage schemes, appearing at a number of public inquiries, for example that at Gedney Drove End in Lincolnshire, and more recently over draining in the Soar Valley in Leicestershire. He has made a number of economic criticisms of the way the benefit of such schemes are calculated, as well as calling for far less secrecy over how the sums are done.

Economic criticisms of the Guidelines are threefold. First, they do not take any account of the risk which is associated with all farming activities. This means that the farmer is paid on the basis of an imaginary crop which is sown perfectly, grows without drought or pest attack, and is harvested without loss. His profit is guaranteed. Second, the requirement on the NCC to cover the cost of the grant the farmer applied for is considerable, as an example calculated by John Bowers in an article in *New Scientist* in February 1983 shows. He looked at an area of grazing marsh which the farmer wanted to convert to arable. Standard figures (such as those in the Wye Farm Pocketbook, an invaluable costing aid) suggest that grazing would have brought in £98 per ha per year. Winter wheat would be worth some £384 per ha, including costs, or £286 per ha more. However, drainage would be needed, at a cost of perhaps £650 per ha. 37.5% of this would be covered by a MAFF grant (£244 per ha), leaving £406 per ha for the farmer to pay over a 20 year period. The annual cost would be £48 per ha (amortised at 10% over 20 years), bringing the net profit from switching to wheat to £238 per ha p.a. This is what the NCC would have to pay the farmer (although in practice factors like the size of his farm and whether he would have to buy new machinery would be taken into account). However, in 1983 the NCC would have been saving MAFF £244 per ha on the drainage grant which is never paid. If this were left out of the calculation, on the basis that the minister ought to refuse grant on an SSSI regardless of the nature of management agreement payments, the cost to the NCC would fall to £210 per ha p.a., a saving of 12%. This may sound little, but on a 500 ha SSSI it would mean a saving of £14 000 per year.

The other major economic criticism of the Guidelines is that the payments include the element of subsidy on agricultural prices. In the same example of the conversion of grazing marsh to arable, 45% of the value of the wheat at the margin is subsidy (as indeed is over half of the value of the beef output). If that subsidy is excluded from the calculation, the extra income for wheat falls to £157 per ha from £286. With drainage costs (allowing for a MAFF grant) of £48 per ha, the extra income falls to £109 per ha. The NCC is paying the difference between £238 per ha (with subsidy) and £109 (without), £129 per ha, which would normally be paid by the EEC Common Agricultural Policy (CAP) agencies. This makes conservation seem far more expensive than it should be, as well as taking money from the conservation budget rather than agriculture's.

Table 6.1 shows a series of calculations done by John Bowers for the NCC in 1984. Column 1 shows the typical cost of annual management agreements on different kinds of land, different farm enterprises, and different proposed developments. Column 2 shows the annual cost to the EEC and the UK government of the proposed change. This includes capital grant. Column 3 shows the difference, which is the real cost of conservation. In the first

Table 6.1 Costs of management agreements and subsidies.

		Typical annual management agreement payment (£ per ha)	Annual cost (£) to government and EEC of proposed development (including drainage and other capital grants)	Real cost of conservation (£)	Saving to government (£)
marshland	Beef cattle to wheat	522	344	+178	0
	Sheep to wheat	480	386	+94	0
	Sheep to wheat	269	264	+5	0
	Sheep to wheat	251	270	−19	19
	Sheep and cattle to wheat and oilseed rape	244	297	−53	53
lowland pasture	Increased dairy stocks	236	734	−518	518
		226	648	−422	422
upland pasture	Increased sheep stocking	35	66	−31	31

Source: Paper by John Bowers to the NCC, 1984. The background to the calculations is given in *The level of protection of UK agriculture* by C. J. Black and J. K. Bowers (1981), University of Leeds, School of Economic Studies Discussion paper no. 99.

three cases (grazing to wheat), this is small, sometimes very small. In the other five, notably those involving the intensification of dairy stocking (important before quotas were introduced in 1984) the costs exceed even the generous calculation of the extra income from improvement as calculated under the guidelines. In these instances management agreement payments are actually cheaper in absolute terms than carrying out the development. It is of course profoundly unreasonable that this money should be spent via the NCC, and hence seem to make conservation more expensive. The fact that if the land were not an SSSI MAFF would encourage the development (and that the farmer would get his profit, paid for by the CAP) says much about the crazy world of agricultural policy and accounting. It makes the detailed provisions of the Guidelines look ridiculous.

Costly cases

The cost of management agreements has probably been the most consistently controversial aspect of the implementation of the Wildlife and Countryside Act. The original Bill had attached to it a financial note suggesting that the NCC would need between £600 000 and £700 000 for land acquisition and management agreements, and indeed this was the figure they received for the financial year 1982/83. However, this estimate took no account of the provision of the Act as it was eventually passed. It also took no account of the vast administrative burden of renotification, nor of the generous terms of the Guidelines when they finally appeared. It was also calculated on the assumption (current in the DOE in 1979) that extra money would only be needed for a small number (30–40) of 'super' SSSIs.

Once the Act was passed, the NCC did its sums, and said that £20 million would be needed over the next 10 years for management agreements. This allowed for agreements over 3000 ha, and the purchase of a further 2000 ha per year, as the Earl of Avon explained to the House of Lords in reply to a question in March 1982. Richard North, writing in the *Observer* in March, commented that 'conservationists have never had confidence in the determined voluntarism of the current scheme, detecting all along the likelihood that there would be little or no money to spare for conservation'. This was indeed a widely held view. The Act, he said 'imposes a machinery on the conservation bodies which it does nothing to finance'. Even the *Field* criticised the shortfall in NCC funding in 1982: 'it needed more money to do its job properly, instead of just doing it'.

There was tangible reason for this concern. For some time the NCC had been involved in negotiations over an area of 140 ha within the Walland Marsh SSSI, on Romney Marsh in Kent. This was grazing land, and the farmer had applied to MAFF for a drainage grant of 40 ha with the intention of converting it to arable. At a meeting in November 1981 attended by all the big guns (Lord Ferrers, Minister of State at MAFF, the Parliamentary Under-Secretary of State at the DOE, the owner of the site and MAFF and DOE officers) the NCC tried to negotiate a management agreement to allow time for more detailed surveys. The owner refused an agreement, but offered to sell the land for £238 000. The NCC Chairman visited the site in person in the new year, with Lord Ferrers and the Director-General, but the owner was still only prepared to sell the land or conclude an agreement at the rate of £400 per ha. A meeting in Whitehall determined that no money should be provided to buy the site, and the NCC decided to withdraw their objection to the drainage.

The outcry from conservationists was immediate. Chris Rose and Charles Secrett published their critique of the Act, *Cash or crisis*, in March 1982, giving full details of the Romney Marsh case, and others. The 1981 Act was, they said, a 'wretched and dishevelled piece of legislation'. They highlighted the cash crisis faced by the NCC, arguing that 'the cash-based conservation system is foundering on a shortage of cash for management agreements'. They argued that the NCC's decision on the Walland Marsh SSSI indicated their refusal to use the full power of the Act, and the government's refusal to put in the money necessary to make it work.

Given the undeniable inflexibility of NCC finances, it is likely that one reason for the NCC's timidity over Walland Marsh was fear that a more important site would be threatened later in the year. This point was tackled by Ian Prestt in a letter to the *Observer* on 21 March. 'It argues it should keep what little money it has in case a more important site becomes endangered. We say it must object loudly when any site is at risk, whether or not it has the money to pay compensation. Only then will the public and Parliament understand that it is the government's failure to produce the cash which is the real cause of the destruction of our wildlife heritage'.

The outcry at the retreat over Romney Marsh may have helped change attitudes within the NCC, particularly in the conservative and landowner-dominated Council itself because in August 1982 they published a statement asserting 'that any of the powers (in the Act) should be used if necessary to further the conservation of any SSSI threatened by a damaging operation'. A few months later they called for a Section 29 Order on Baddesley Common in Hampshire.

This tougher stance, or rather the decision actually to use the powers given by the Act, did not alter the basic problem that there was too little money for management agreements. This only really changed after a commitment was wrung from the Secretary of State for the Environment on a visit to the Somerset Levels in spring 1983 that the government would provide all the money necessary for management agreements on SSSIs. The Levels had become a considerable problem as relations between the farmers and the NCC deteriorated. The value of parts of the Levels for conservation, particularly West Sedgemoor had long been known. However, it was not formally made an SSSI until March 1982, although it had been treated as such since 1977 by MAFF, who had consulted the NCC over grant applications. Despite intense ministerial pressure on the NCC to reduce the area of the SSSI, 1010 ha were notified, the full extent of that recommended by the NCC's scientists. The notification letter caused offence among farmers, and a CLA report in June 1982 challenged the notification. There was a series of public meetings, and eventually the chairman of the NCC and the Regional Officer were burned in effigy. The Act's provisions seemed inadequate, and the whole notion of consensus was at risk. Hence the Secretary of State's visit, and his statement that the government would meet the bill for management agreements, so that farmers would not suffer. This promise has been repeated at various times ever since.

Attention then shifted to the size of payments being made, or at

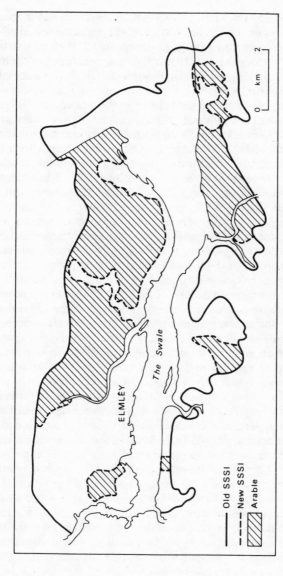

Figure 6.1 Shrinkage of the Swale sssi in Kent: areas excluded when the boundary of the sssi was redrawn in 1982.

ELMLEY

The Swale

0   1   2
      km

—— Old SSSI
---- New SSSI
▨ Arable

least discussed. The first to hit the headlines concerned the Swale Estuary in Kent. The Swale SSSI covers about 6000 ha, of which 165 ha is an NNR and 270 ha an RSPB reserve. The SSSI was first scheduled as long ago as 1951, but as successive farmers have drained the grazing marsh and ploughed it up the boundary has flexed and shrunk (Fig. 6.1). Overall the area of grazing marsh in North Kent has fallen by 48%. In 1977 the SSSI was amended to include an area called Elmley Island, and the site was included in the Nature Conservation Review. In 1973 an area of some 800 ha, on Elmley Island, owned by the Oxford University Chest, was let to a new tenant. He saw the possibility of developing the poor sheep pasture for arable. In 1981 he ploughed 101 ha of higher land of little scientific interest. In April 1982 he proposed a major programme of underdrainage to bring a further 463 ha under arable over three years. Discussions began of a management agreement over the land, and articles in the press in March 1983 announced that the farmer was likely to become a millionaire within 10 years on the basis of compensation payments. These rumours were roundly dismissed in farming journals, and the disclosure discomforted the NCC because the owner concerned was actually interested in managing the land positively for conservation, not sitting back and banking his money. However, the figures were not wholly unrealistic. Calculations showed that the conversion from sheep to wheat might be worth an extra £220 per ha (indeed possibly up to £480 per ha), or £102 000 over the whole farm per year. The prospect of a million pounds out of the NCC's budget in 10 years for just one part of one SSSI was real enough to worry many observers. In the event negotiations over the area dragged on to reach a Section 16 Agreement to declare the area an NNR under the 1949 Act, but the payments remained substantial. In addition, other farms in a similar position sought similar arrangements. One agreement for 21 years was made in 1982 over less than 50 ha at just under £249 per ha. These expenses obviously drove a coach and horses through the NCC's estimate of the cost of agreements.

The second case which caught the public eye concerned Boulsbury Wood, part of Cranborne Chase on the Hampshire/Dorset border. Surveys revealed its importance for nature conservation in 1982, by which time a substantial area had been planted with conifers. Notification of an area of 145 ha began in 1982, as did negotiation of a management agreement. In June 1983 an article in *New Scientist* stated that the owner would be paid £20 000 per year (£138 per ha) (index linked, of course) over 65 years to maintain the broadleaved woodland of the site. Again, this revelation caused acute embarrassment, but again the figure was not far out. A short term agreement in 1983 on a small area involved a small lump sum payment and an annual payment at just under £150 per hectare.

These cases although widely publicised, were not unique. The number of management agreements concluded under S15 of the Act rose from 111 in the year ending March 1983 to 139 in 1983/84, and 220 in the year 1984/85 (Fig. 6.2). The cost increased fourfold to £206 000 p.a. from 1953 to 1984, and again to £948 000 in 1984/85. An enormous backlog of sites under negotiation was also building up, a great many involving substantial cost. By the end of March 1985, 132 agreements and 60 short term agreements had been concluded since the Act was passed. Some were nominal – a few pounds per ha, or a lump sum of a few tens of pounds to a conservation-minded owner. A number involved far larger payments. Among the more notorious was the payment of £0.25 million for a 99 year nature reserve agreement over Blair Nam Faoileag in Caithness, which had been threatened with afforestation. Another site in the news was the Halvergate SSSI on the Bure Marshes in Norfolk, where a 21 year annual agreement over about 40 ha cost over £500 per ha p.a. Other meadow and pasture sites threatened with development were also protected by agreements, at rates of between £100 and £500 per ha, often for agreements of two or three years, and usually for small portions of five hectares or less in one ownership within a larger SSSI. The overall costs to the NCC were therefore not large, but neither was the whole area protected. For example, six agreements in 1984 for periods of a year or less over a total of 42 ha of Derwent Ings in Humberside, a flood meadow site, involved lump sum payments of almost £8000. Clearly predictions about the punitive cost of the Act and the guidelines, once dismissed as alarmist, were being borne out in practice.

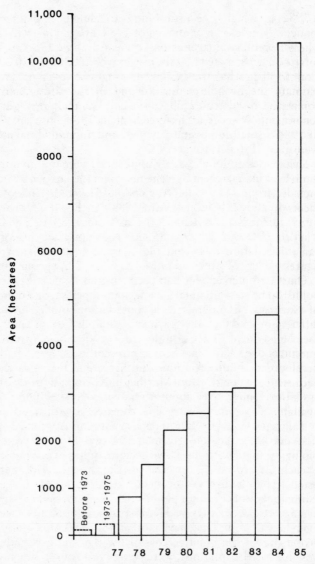

Figure 6.2 The area of land subject to NCC management agreements under Section 15 of the Countryside Act 1968.

The bill for the Act

There have been relatively few attempts to calculate the likely total cost of management agreements under the Wildlife and Countryside Act, even though it is now widely held that the estimate of £15–25 million made in 1982 is too low. The fact is confirmed by the additional grant of £7 million specifically for renotification and site safeguard made to the NCC in the autumn of 1984. Even at that time, however, both the NCC and the DOE were guessing. In March 1985, the Secretary of State announced a review of the guidelines by agricultural economics consultant Laurence Gould, to be completed by the end of June. This was to include an assessment of the likely cost of management agreements on SSSIs over the next 10 years. At the time of writing (July 1985) this has not been made public, and indeed it is not clear whether the conclusions will be released at all. Until they are, one can at best produce rather crude approximations of the expected figures.

One approach, tried in the report *Implementing the act*, published by the World Wildlife Fund and the British Association of Nature Conservationists in 1984, works from the area of different kinds of habitat and likely costs of payments to maintain them. Such calculations are open to all sorts of criticism: they beg questions about the size of holdings, the suitability of land for development and many other things. They are also difficult because, unbelievably, very basic information about the area of SSSIs throughout Britain and the amount of each habitat is not available. None the less, some crude calculations are possible.

Taking the number of SSSIs listed in the Rayner Review of the NCC in the spring of 1983 (4150), of which 76% were of biological interest, and assuming that the proportion of the area of each site in each habitat type was the same as in the 'key sites' listed in the Nature Conservation Review, it was possible to estimate the area of each habitat in the whole system. Setting low average figures of the amount of compensation per hectare on the main habitats (like lowland grassland and woodland), in order to give a conservative figure, it was then possible to calculate the possible total cost of management agreements on *all* SSSIs in the whole biological SSSI system. The total was £42.8 million per

Table 6.2 The possible annual cost of agreements on all biological sssis, May 1985.

	%	Estimated area (million ha)	Est Comp per ha (£)	Estimated annual cost (£)
woodland	27	0.43	50	23.5 m
lowland grassland	19	0.30	100	30.0m
coast	17	0.27	0	0
peat	13	0.21	30	6.3 m
open water	12	0.19	0	0
uplands	12	0.19	20	3.8m
				61.6m

5899 sssis listed for notification and renotification May 1985, 4483 (76%) of biological interest. Estimated average area 354 ha each = total 1.59 million ha of biological importance.

year, about a thousand times the figure actually spent by the NCC in the year 1982–3. This figure is fairly staggering, but it refers to the situation in 1983. By June 1985, a total of 78 sssis had been renotified. If the same figures are reworked, using the more recent estimate of 354 ha per site given in the 1984 publication *Nature conservation in Great Britain*, the total rises to £61.6 million per year (Table 6.2).

As an order of magnitude estimate of the cost of protecting the *whole* of the sssi system this is interesting, indeed shocking. However, it disregards the question of how many sssis will need agreements, and their real cost. One can get at these by another method, using data on agreements already concluded, plus more judicious guesswork. By the end of the 1984/5 financial year, data on over 500 agreements were available, either Section 15 agreements over sssis or Section 16 Nature Reserve Agreements. As explained above, some were cheap and some were expensive. The average cost was about £45 per ha, although the number of large sums included might make that rather a high average for estimation purposes. To provide some kind of maximum and minimum figures, one could use £45 and £30 per ha.

Table 6.3 shows the results of these calculations. The cost of

Table 6.3 Estimated annual costs of management agreements in sssis

Area (million ha)		Agreement cost	
		At £45 per ha	At £30 per ha
2.0	all sssis	£90.0 m	£60.0 m
1.52	biological sssis	£68.4 m	£45.6 m
1.0	assuming one third area is worthless mountain or coast, or is owned by conservation agencies	£45.0 m	£30.0 m
0.66	assuming only two thirds of sssis on valuable land need agreements	£29.7 m	£19.8 m

agreements over the whole sssi system (probably 2 million ha) might be between £60 million (at £30 per ha) and £90 million (at £45 per ha). If one takes only the 76% of sssis of biological interest, to make a direct comparison with the previous estimate, the figure lies between £46 million and £68 million. This suggests that the previous figure may not be unrealistic. However, this ignores the fact that a significant amount of sssi land is owned by one conservation agency or another, and some is of no conceivable commercial value, being mountain top land (presumably not wanted for ski piste development) or unreclaimable coast. The NCC estimates that one third of the area of sssis may be in these categories and not need management agreements. This brings the costs down to between £30 million and £45 million per year. On top of this one might speculate that only two thirds of the owner–occupiers will want agreements in the forseeable future. This brings the figure down again to between £20 million and £30 million per year.

These figures are extremely crude. They ignore, for example, the fact that up to 10% of agreements will be on a lump sum basis, and may be at lower cost, and they do not take into account the lag effect of slow progress with renotification. This means it may be some years before any of these theoretical figures are attained. On the other hand, they ignore the very considerable costs (in terms of extra manpower, time and travel) of negotiating agreements and revising them, and the expenses of the owner or occupier's surveyor and solicitor which the NCC pays, and the payments of arrears on agreements which have taken a long time to conclude. All these will push the real cost of agreements up. These factors may balance, or may raise or lower the cost of the agreements. It is possible to be a lot more complicated in estimating them, as doubtless DOE's consultants will be, but they are essentially trivial in comparison either with the projected totals, or the assumptions used to derive them.

There is nothing magical about these figures, and little that is certain. One can be fairly sure that the cost of agreements will rise to £20 million per year at the very least within two or three years. It is quite likely to be £30 or £40 million and could very well be more. Even the lowest of these figures involves a doubling of the NCC's grant-in-aid for 1984/5, exceeds the 1985/6 budget by almost a third and is equivalent to its total budget for 1986/7 (£32.1 million). It remains to be seen what figures the DOE's consultants themselves suggest, but it is unlikely to be much different. It will be extremely interesting to see how the DOE respond to their report. They might try to argue with the Treasury that the extra money is worth it; it is, after all, but a drop in the ocean compared to the agriculture budget and substitutes directly for part of that budget. Another possibility is that the DOE will seek to reduce the cost of management agreements for site protection by streamlining the Financial Guidelines.

There are two possible procedural changes to the Guidelines which would have a significant impact on the renotification process (especially the backlog of agreements) and possibly on the cost. The first is to adopt *Standard Payments* widely. These are allowed for in the Guidelines, and involve uniform payments per ha for particular categories of land use change. Thus a certain sum might be set for the conversion of grazing marsh to arable, based (as in any individual case) on the profit foregone. The big advantage here is speed, as the Guidelines state 'the use of standard sums in this way may be found convenient by both parties, since the need for detailed assessment of a proposed operation is eliminated, and agreement can therefore be reached more quickly'. Under the present Guidelines the farmer can opt to be individually assessed, and Standard Payments have only so far been tried in the Berwyn Mountains in Wales. With suitable backing from farming organisations they could be adopted more widely, and would certainly reduce the delay in concluding agreements. They would do little for the overall cost unless the farmer's freedom to opt out were removed.

The other approach, perhaps more likely to be adopted is to adopt a *Flat Rate Payment*. This is similar to that payable in the Norfolk Broads in the experimental scheme introduced in 1985 by MAFF and the CC, but not identical. Basically an average national figure could be set for each type of land, based (rather notionally) on its potential for development. Farmers could receive this without having to go through the PDO notification procedure. Although it would certainly represent in most cases a less attractive option than the present arrangement, it would have the advantage of simplicity and speed, and would be fairer since sympathetic farmers with no desire to damage SSSIs could also receive it. If the rates were set appropriately, it is possible (but by no means certain) that money could be saved.

The former of these two options is far more likely to be adopted than the second, because opposition to it from farmers and farming organisations is likely to be less. If it were seen as a way of preserving the voluntary principle, it might receive some support. Both alternatives would be easier to introduce than anything which tackled the basis of the Guidelines themselves. One option here is to abandon annual payments altogether, and return to Lord Porchester's original notion for Exmoor of lump sum payments reflecting loss of the capital value of the land because of the restriction of operations. This would probably reduce the cost of SSSI protection, although possibly not the complexity of calculating payments, but if implemented would have a high political cost. The DOE is unlikely to move in this direction at present: indeed, their consultants would be unlikely to suggest it. The DOE, and the Conservative government, is probably too deeply committed to the success of the voluntary principle to abandon it altogether. Currently, therefore, more radical options, such as a move away from compensation towards planning control, are not on the table for consideration. The DOE would also find it difficult at present to refuse to give the

NCC the money it needs for agreements, as they did in 1982, although it is not inconceivable that they might try. Future possibilities are discussed in the final chapter. Overshadowing the whole debate, however, are the twin monoliths of agricultural and forestry policy. Both are backed by gigantic budgets compared to that devoted to conservation, and both are largely beyond the control of influence of the DOE. They are the key to any future conservation policy in this country.

Money for agriculture

The most significant practical shortcoming with the Act and the Financial Guidelines, concerns not their internal workings (although obviously the problems here are considerable) but their complete inadequacy in the face of government financial support for agricultural intensification and afforestation. These two land uses have gradually emerged as the foremost agents of habitat loss in the countryside, although they are by no means the only ones. As Chapter 1 argued, the nature of both activities has been changing over the past 200 years, increasingly in response to government policy. Since World War II the rate of change in both agriculture and forestry has been drastic, and with it has gone significant reduction in the amount of wildlife habitat in the countryside. It was primarily these losses which the 1981 Act ostensibly sought to stop. It is clear that the provisions are inadequate.

In the case of agriculture, the reason is simple: the new money being pumped into management agreements to preserve areas of semi-natural habitat is set in direct opposition to the vastly larger sum in the agriculture budget designed to encourage the development of those areas in the search for greater efficiency and higher output. There is a saying among systems analysts that all good systems run downhill: the 1981 Act's management agreements do not. They are pushing uphill with relatively small sums pitted against the mighty budget of the CAP and MAFF.

Funding for British agriculture comes from both the EEC, through the CAP, and direct from the British government. In Britain, for example, the Agriculture and Horticulture Grants

Scheme (largely closed down by MAFF in July 1985) was not funded by the CAP, nor is the work of the Agricultural Research Council. About two thirds of all EEC spending goes into the CAP through the European Agricultural Guidance and Guarantee Fund, generally known by its slightly more mellifluous French acronym FEOGA. Of FEOGA's money, 96% goes into the guarantee section which controls the market price of agricultural commodities in Europe. The rest is channelled into the guidance section where it is used to influence the economic and social structure of agriculture in the community.

CAP price support involves a number of mechanisms. Producers of some commodities receive a premium if the actual market price falls below that the EEC Agricultural Ministers set, in others there is support buying on the open market to raise the market price. Surplus food – which cannot be sold at all – is bought by intervention boards and stored, creating the various wine, oil or milk lakes and butter or grain mountains which have become such an embarrassment to governments. Some is dumped at cheap prices on the international market, some got rid of as food aid to the Third World. Meanwhile import levies are charged on food imported into the EEC to raise it to the fixed price, to the fury of other over-producers such as the USA who are thus robbed of a place to dump their own surpluses. In 1982 expenditure under the guarantee section was £6921 million, rising to over £8 billion the following year. While the CAP is the only effective approach towards the principle of a common market, its costs, and the chronic surpluses have brought a number of political crises and near disaster for the community on several occasions in 1984 and 1985.

The structural polices of the CAP involve far less money, but are also important. Some directives, such as that encouraging small farmers to retire so that their land can be amalgamated into larger holdings, have little effect in Britain, whose own policies effectively forced small farmers out of business long ago. Others are important in Britain, for example FEOGA pays 25% of the cost of capital grants awarded under Britain's Agriculture and Horti-culture Development Scheme (not to be confused with the similarly named grants scheme which is not EEC funded). In 1980 and 1981 Britain took between 30% and 40% of FEOGA's expenditure in the area. Also extremely important in Britain is the Less Favoured Area's (LFA's) Directive which is intended to assist farmers in areas severely constrained by adverse climate or poor soil. Since Britain has (in Continental terms) no real mountains, this has been taken to apply to hill farming areas in upland England, Wales and extensive areas of Scotland. Britain takes between 20% and 30% of FEOGA's expenditure on this, involving in 1982 some £18m in grants.

Detailed critiques of the CAP require considerable economic expertise and a machievellian taste for complexity. MAFF data for the past five years of expenditure on different aspects of agriculture, from the 1985 *Annual review of agriculture*, are given in Table 6.4. The total has fluctuated between just below £1000 million in 1981/82 to over £1700 million in 1983/84 and almost £1800 million (projected) 1984/85. Obviously inflation is a factor here, but the increase is still notable. Market regulation has been the biggest element in this, but capital support, which has done so much to transform British agriculture and the British

Table 6.4 The cost of British agriculture (£ million).

	1980/1	1981/2	1982/3	1983/4	1984/5 (forecast)
market regulation under CAP	648.3	678.6	1099.1	1374.5	1424.1
price guarantees	45.5	17.1	8.1	9.9	3.4
capital support (in AHGS AHDS)	205.1	173.9	206.0	220.6	205.1
agricultural support in special areas (inc. LFA)	113.5	102.8	119.6	123.5	137.2
Milk Outgoers Scheme	0	0	0	0	10.0
Total	1012.4	972.4	1432.8	1728.5	1779.8
FEOGA receipts (total)	606.3 (60%)	742.4 (76%)	804.8 (56%)	1200.3 (69%)	1139.7 (64%)

Source: Annual Review of Agriculture HMSO.

162

countryside, has also been substantial at around £200 million every year. Of this money between 56% and 76% has in the past come from FEOGA, but of course in the long run this is paid for by member countries, and since Britain is still (despite years of production-promoting policies) a net importer of food, she pays a large part of this.

These figures ignore a number of other inputs into the development of the landscape by agriculture: notably perhaps payments for land drainage which have featured so strongly in recent cases of threats to SSSIs. In 1983/4 these amounted to £31.6 million, plus investments by international drainage boards. This is perhaps a reasonable figure on which to base a comparison between the scale of support for intensive agriculture, and that for conservation. This figure, for land drainage alone, is of the same order as that which *may* be paid for conservation management agreements. The total financial backing for agriculture is far greater: £1700 million versus perhaps (at a most optimistic guess) £50 million. The possible scale of payments for conservation is just 3% of that for agriculture. The *actual* expenditure in 1983/4 on management agreements was £207 000. This is about 0.01% of the money put into agriculture, a trivial proportion. The imbalance is enormous. Expecting this conservation money to stop damage to semi-natural habitats by agriculture is like trying to stop a tank with a peashooter.

The Act, and the Guidelines, are attacking symtoms not causes. They are an attempt to prevent some of the adverse effects of agricultural policy without changing that policy itself, and as such they cannot really be expected to be very successful.

Forestry's fairyland

Forestry in Britain is also backed by far greater financial resources than are likely to be mobilised in management agreements under the Wildlife and Countryside Act to protect existing habitats. Forestry activity in Britain is split between the FC itself and private woodland owners. Most of the FC's activity is in the uplands, and their planting is of conifers. It has included extensive afforestation of hill land in Scotland, most controversially in the far North in Sutherland and Caithness and in windy western districts where there is a high risk of trees blowing down before reaching maturity. Private forestry is more evenly split between conifers (new planting) and broadleaves (in existing woodlands) and includes a larger proportion of lowland woodlands. In October 1984 there were some 572 000 ha of conifers and 544 000 ha of broadleaved woodland and coppice in private woodlands, plus what the FC statistics dismiss as 'unproductive woodland' amounting to 163 000 ha. A large amount of this woodland is of high nature conservation value. In terms of direct expenditue, FC grants to private woodland owners (plus a few for research, etc.) amounted to £5.8 million in 1983/84. Gross expenditure on all FC forests was £107.2 million, of which £48.7 million was recouped in timber sales. The net direct cost of FC forestry was therefore £58.5 million in the year 1983/84. Britain produces less than 9% of home timber needs, on a similar proportion (9.4%) of the surface area of the country. Much of that timber is of poor quality, suitable only for pulping.

The cost of timber production on the poor and hilly land which forms the bulk of the FC's holding and new private forestry is high. There is a large element of government subsidy therefore in all expenditure on British forestry. The most marked support, however, is to private forestry because the only return to the exchequer is the rather nominal tax on eventual timber sales. It is here that the scales are most heavily weighted against nature conservation. Part of this support comes through direct FC grants on approved planting in private woodlands. In 1983–4 private planting amounted to just under 20 000 ha of which 18 000 ha was of conifers. FC grants on this land probably amounted to about £4.9 million on conifers and £0.9 million on broadleaved planting. Grant was therefore worth about £272 per ha of coniferous planting, to cover perhaps the first 10 years of a plantation's life.

The real element of government (and hence taxpayer) support for private forestry, however, does not concern direct grants, but indirect tax benefits. These favour in particular anyone paying a high rate of income tax, enabling them to treat the costs of establishing a forestry plantation as a tax-deductable allowance. What was (presumably) intended as a policy to encourage

164

appropriate tree planting by ordinary landowners has become an irresistible investment attraction to those with extremely large incomes and high tax ratings. Many of these have had no previous interest in landownership or management, and their interest in forestry is purely that of financial profit, not woodmanship. People with high earning potential over short periods, such as professional sportsmen and entertainers, are especially attracted to investment in new planting because it provides a way of capitalising their income. A number of consultancy and management companies have sprung up or expanded to meet the needs of such people. The largest of these are Fountain Forestry, the Economic Forestry Group and Tilhill, but there are others.

The calculation works out as follows. Planting on typical hill land might cost £1000 per ha. Under the FC's Forestry Grant Scheme 1981 a payment of £230 per ha against establishment costs (fencing, roads, etc.) is likely, bringing the net cost of establishment to £770. Under Schedule D it is possible to offset 60% of this against tax, bringing the net cost down to £308 per ha. The total public subsidy, including tax, is £692 per ha. However, the tax benefits to the private forester do not end there. Once the plantation is established, annual costs fall and the advantages decline. It is then possible to sell the land (to a close relative, or a company established for the purpose) at which point taxation can switch back to Schedule B. Under this, tax is paid on one third of the unimproved value of the land, but not on the timber itself. The timber can later be sold tax free. Very little money therefore goes back into the public purse. The large element of public subsidy in the establishment of a new plantation which is owned by a high-rate taxpayer is shown in Table 6.5, as is the effect of subsequent purchase by an investment company. For the sake of simplicity these figures do not show how costs are discounted over time, but in fact this makes little difference to the importance of public subsidy.

The financial implication of these possibilities will obviously vary with the situation of individual investors, but the large element of government subsidy is clear. Clear too is the attractiveness of the package. This is demonstrated by the fact that some owners have felt able to dispense with the planting grants

Table 6.5 Forestry finance: an estimate of government subsidy and private profit in a plantation of Sitka Spruce, over the first 15 years.[1]

(a) Owned by high-rate taxpayer(Schedule D tax)

	Cost per hectare
cost of land purchase	(£560)
cost of establishment	(£1000)
Forestry Commission planting grant	£230
pre-tax cost of establishment	(£770)
sum on which the relief payable	£770
tax relief (60%)	£462
cost net of tax	(£868)
value of plantation at 15 years	£1800
profit per ha[2]	£932
cost to Exchequer (grant and tax)	£692 (74%)

(b) Bought by investment company

	Price per hectare
purchase price of plantation	(£1800)
value of thinnings (15–35 years)	£2000
value clear felled timber	£7000
sale of bare land	£560
gross profit	£7760
less cost of capitalized maintenance	£1200
net profit per ha	£6560
benefit to Exchequer	nominal tax on land value

[1] No account has been taken in this example of the discounting of costs over time.

[2] Excluding cost of mortgage to buy land.

and still hope to profit substantially. The profit here is almost entirely through tax advantages, the quality or saleability of the timber being quite irrelevant. What has happened is that land has been planted without approval from the FC. Such approval is voluntary, but is necessary for grant aid. In April 1985 planting began on an 800 ha property in the Lammermuir Hills south of Edinburgh without such approval, and in May Tilhill Forestry Ltd. planted 230 ha without permission near Carter Bar in the Borders region. This caused consternation at the FC, and presumably alarm at the Department of Agriculture who had opposed the planting. Grant is obviously not necessary to make afforestation attractive to potential investors. There is also the added advantage that hill land without planting approval is considerably cheaper to buy than that with approval: in mid 1984 hill land was worth £260 per ha, planting land £560 per ha. That £300 difference more than offsets the lost £230 grant per ha, especially as tax relief is still allowed on the full planting costs. The profitable nature of planting without grant is shown in Table 6.6. The level of public subsidy is again high.

Attention has been most closely focused of late on the activities of the forestry companies. The financial support for afforestation, combined with their entrepreneurial skill at finding high rate taxpayers keen to invest in forestry and owners willing to sell land, has shown the 1981 Act's provisions to protect SSSIs to be inadequate. The first major case concerned Creaig Meagaidh in Invernesshire. This mountain stands above Glen Spean, and contained a large SSSI on the basis of the range of habitats represented in the rise from the floor of the Glen (albeit flooded by a hydro-electric reservoir) to the mountain communities of the summit. The site was one of those included in the 1977 Nature Conservation Review. Fountain Forestry brought 4000 ha of the estate at £75 per ha (total £300 000), and proposed to plant an extensive area. The NCC objected to grant aid for planting, but the FC supported it. The matter was referred to the Secretary of State for Scotland. He proposed a compromise which pleased neither party: Fountain Forestry could go ahead and plant half the site (530 ha) with a grant of £120 000. The NCC continued to object and eventually Fountain Forestry agreed to sell the land to the NCC for £430 000 without planting, making a substantial

Table 6.6 The profitability of planting land with and without forestry clearance.[1]

	Planting approval (£/ha)	No planting approval (£/ha)
cost of land	£560	£260
cost of establishing plantation (Sitka Spruce)	£1000	£1000
planting grant	£230	0
pre-tax cost	£770	£1000
sum on which tax relief is payable	£770	£1000
tax relief	£462	£600
cost net of tax	£868	£660
value of plantation	£1800	£1800
profit[2]	£932	£1140
cost to Exchequer	632 (68%)	600 (53%)

Notes [1] No account has been taken on this example of the discounting of costs over time.
[2] Excludes cost of mortgage to buy land.

profit thereby. In due course Creag Meagaidh will be declared an NNR.

As an example of the confusion and waste engendered by land use policy in Britain, Creag Meagaidh cannot be bettered. It demonstrates the inadequacy of the 1981 Act's provision to protect SSSIs of this sort against the concerns of forestry interests. In the end the only way to protect the site was by purchase, an expensive alternative open to the NCC long before the Act was passed. Even this was only possible because Fountain Forestry agreed to sell: any application for a CPO would have had to be approved by the Secretary of State for Scotland, who had already approved grant-aided afforestation. More recently Fountain Forestry has been in the news again, being criticised for the nature and scale of its investments in Sutherland and Caithness. A series of articles by the journalist Melanie Reed in the *Scotsman* in 1984 and 1985 highlighted its activities which produce remarkably little benefit to local communities. It seems it owns or manages somewhere between 20 000 and 30 000 ha of land of which it is planting 12 000 ha, mostly with Sitka spruce and lodgepole Pine. This enormous area (two thirds of the area of all private planting 1983–84) is said to have cost the government (in grants and tax benefits for Fountain's clients) £6 million, or £500 per ha. There are doubts (dismissed by Fountain) about whether the trees will grow well enough to be economic on the poor soil without suffering severe windthrow damage. There are doubts too about the wisdom of planting Lodgepole pine, which has been extensively damaged by pine beauty moth on the FC's own Scottish plantations, requiring costly and undesirable spraying with the organophosphorus pesticide fenitrothion, among others. To add insult to injury, Fountain Forestry have ploughed up part of Strathy Bog National Nature Reserve. The *Scotsman* concluded in an editorial in October 1984 'forestry policy is ripe for a searching review'. Forestry is certainly beyond the power of the NCC to control using the provisions of the 1981 Act.

Money for conservation

Against the weight of government support for agriculture and forestry, there are relatively few financial aids in the NCC's armoury to protect SSSIs. One is taxation. Capital Transfer Tax (CTT) was introduced in the Finance Act 1975, and one exemption was allowed to owners of land of 'outstanding scientific, scenic or historic interest', managed by agreement with the Treasury based on advice from a government conservation agency. The CC has used this extensively for scenic land, and has dealt with about 500 applications since 1975. The NCC has used it far less, only handling 100 cases since 1975, mostly small areas. One difficulty was that the provisions applied only to landowners, not tenants, another that the Treasury took a long time to accept the NCC's 1976 recommendation that all SSSIs should qualify for CTT exemption. In the event, the 1981 Act makes management agreements potentially so lucrative for landowners, that CTT exemption becomes rather irrelevant. None the less, there is clearly potential in developing tax legislation to favour

169

conservation and help redress the balance *vis-à-vis* agriculture and forestry. In 1985 the Landscape Institute produced a report *Farmed landscapes and a balanced future* which recommended an extensive system of tax relief (and management payments) for farmers who register their land, and manage it in a certain way. The proposal is complicated, but the idea has obvious interest. Another simple suggestion is that the 10% tax relief 'douceuer' enjoyed by landowners who sell land to the NCC and the National Trust (among other bodies) should be extended to voluntary nature conservation organisations. Small improvements in the position of nature conservation are possible by mechanisms of this sort, but the overall effect is unlikely to be very significant.

A potentially much more exciting source of funds for conservation is the agricultural budget itself. This is possible under two Directives of the EEC, part of the structural policy side of FEOGA's work. The best known is the Less Favoured Areas Directive. This was originally made in 1975, to provide assistance for farmers who suffered particular handicaps. This chiefly meant environmental handicaps, but the Directive specifically included 'small areas affected by specific handicaps and in which farming must be continued in order to conserve the countryside and to preserve the tourist potential of the area or in order to protect the coastline'. Farmers in LFAs receive Hill Livestock Compensatory Allowances on every head of livestock and higher rates of capital grants for capital works such as land drainage, or pasture reseeding.

Although other EEC governments (notably Holland) interpreted this Directive so as to provide support for farmers in areas of high environmental value, the Ministry of Agriculture in Britain has refused to do this. In Britain the LFA Directive has therefore been used to contribute to the general direction of agricultural policy, towards intensification and increased production, and not as an instrument to integrate conservation and agriculture. None the less, as the Dutch experience shows, the potential is there. In March 1985 the Directive was revised, and the new wording makes specific mention of payments 'in order to ensure the conservation of the environment'. This should make it easier to use it to embrace nature conservation, but it is not clear whether MAFF will agree to use it in this way.

However, a new article in the EEC structures regulation in March 1985 is of direct importance to nature conservation. Article 19 introduces the idea of 'environmentally sensitive areas' (dubbed ESAs instantly) which are 'particular areas of recognised importance from an ecological and landscape point of view'. The Article allows member states to introduce national schemes in these areas 'in order to contribute towards the introduction or continued use of agricultural production practices compatible with the requirements of conserving the natural habitat and ensuring an inadequate income for farmers'. The initiative for this article was British, MAFF's response to the growing furor over the agriculture and conservation 'crisis'. Lord Belstead announced it in the summer of 1984 (following the highly critical Lords report on EEC Agricultural Structures), but like a lot of British suggestions in Brussels it was regarded with intense suspicion. However, after much manoeuvring it was passed. The British government introduced enabling legislation in the Agriculture Bill, debated in the House of Commons in November 1985. The real question now is how MAFF intends to interpret the article, and how it envisages the ESAS. One idea is that *all* SSSIs are ESAs by definition, and indeed one view of the EC's decision to adopt the article is that it is to legalise the British payments for management agreements on SSSIs. Another view of ESAs is that because SSSIs are covered by existing safeguards they should be areas outside current designations, probably far more extensive than most SSSIs. MAFF apparently takes this view, and proposed only half a dozen ESAs initially. In October 1985, the CC and NCC produced a list of 46 possible areas, including all 10 national parks, and a further 17 were expected from the CC for Scotland. A revised list of thirteen 'priority areas' was drawn up early in 1986. In theory the ESAs, described by *The Economist* in September 1985 as 'Eurosense', are exciting. ESA flat rate payments could largely take over from management agreements in some areas, and could provide a basis for bringing together different kinds of landscape designations (e.g. scenic or historical) on common ground for the first time. It remains to be seen whether they will fulfil their potential.

Some indication of official thinking is given by developments in the Halvergate Marshes in Norfolk. This area in the valley of the

River Bure has been consistently in the headlines since 1982. It contains a substantial sssi, but in fact most of the controversy has concerned the scenic importance of a wider area, and the attempts of the Broads Authority to prevent its conversion from grazing marsh to arable. In the spring of 1984 William Waldegrave made his famous rash promise to the Commons that Halvergate was safe for a year, then further ploughing, sit-ins by FOE and a blaze of media attention followed. In the spring of 1985 a more permanent solution was found, on the lines of Article 19. On 15 March MAFF and the CC announced the Broads Grazing Marshes Scheme. This will run until 1988, with a budget of £1.7 million, half coming from MAFF. Farmers agreeing to maintain livestock grazing at between 0.5 and 1.5 livestock units per acre (i.e. one cow or rather more bullocks or heifers) and to take only one cut of hay or silage will receive a payment of £50 per acre (£123 per ha). Take up of the scheme has apparently been good.

Obviously, the size of the agriculture budget is such that if (and it is a big if) MAFF is serious about diverting money towards 'environmentally sensitive agriculture', the potential benefit for conservation is high. The LFA Directive allows MAFF and the Department of Agriculture and Fisheries for Scotland to do it in the uplands (although to date MAFF has ignored this). Article 19 allows a number of attractive avenues for action. However, a huge amount depends on MAFF's own view of their policy objectives, and indeed about the sharing of responsibilities with the DOE. About such matters one can at the moment only speculate. At the very least, the sharp debate about how many ESAs are defined and how large they are, is likely to continue. Indeed, in January 1986 the Exmoor National Park Officer criticised MAFF's decision to allocate only £6 million for ESA payments, which would mean that only its preferred total of six areas would be designated. Many people active in the countryside will be sorry to see yet another tier of designations descend, but the prospects for the use of ESAs are exciting. However, in this, as well as the more destructive aspects of agricultural policy, the future of areas of conservation importance depends far less on the slight protection afforded by the 1981 Act than on other policies for the countryside which are little influenced by conservation. In this respect the 1981 Act has brought little change.

Further reading

Adams, W. 1984. *Implementing the Act: a study of habitat protection under Part II of the Wildlife and Countryside Act*. Oxford: British Association of Nature Conservationists.

Body, R. 1984. *Farming in the clouds*. London: Temple Smith.

Body, R. 1985. British agricultural policy since the Second World War. *Agric. Hist. Rev.* 33(1), 66–76.

Bowers, J. K. 1983. How conservation will bankrupt the conservationists. *New Scientist* 10 February 1983, 357.

Bowers, J. K. 1983. Cost–benefit analysis of wetland drainage. *Environment and Planning* A 15, 227–35.

Bowers, J. K. 1983. Economics and conservation: the case of land drainage. In *Conservation in perspective*, A. Warren and F. B. Goldsmith (eds), pp. 329–52. London: Wiley.

Bowers, J. and P. Cheshire 1983. *Agriculture, the countryside and land use*. London: Methuen.

Clout, H. 1984. *A rural policy for the EEC?* London: Methuen.

Grove, R. 1983. *The future for forestry*. Oxford: British Association of Nature Conservationists.

Howarth, R. 1985. *Farming for farmers? A critique of agricultural support policy*. London: Institute of Economic Affairs.

Landscape Institute. 1985. *Farmed landscapes and a balanced future*. London: The Landscape Institute.

Moore, P. 1985. The real world of private forestry. *ECOS* 6(2), 2–7.

Moore, P. 1985. The unacceptable face of private forestry. *ECOS* 6(4), 39–40.

Chapter Seven

The conservation of nature

Changing policies

Almost the whole of the complex network of policies relating to nature conservation and natural habitats is in a state of flux. This is most obviously true of conservation, which in the four years since the 1981 Act has enjoyed two Private Members' Bills, one House of Commons Environment Committee Inquiry, and an inordinate number of headlines, editorials and leading articles. One might be pardoned for thinking that this reflected an unequivocal consensus, and that the official action needed was both well understood and widely accepted. Despite the effective work of Wildlife Link in co-ordinating the voluntary bodies, and signs of increasing dynamism from the NCC, this is unfortunately not the case. There are too many new ideas to make the road ahead for conservation completely clear. None the less the inadequacy of some routes is obvious. A great deal will depend on developments in related policy areas.

The most significant area affecting conservation is of course agriculture. Agricultural policy has come under sustained attack in recent years: as a leader in *The Times* put it in January 1985, 'its achievements lie almost forgotten behind the appearances of misdirected effort in the production of unsaleable surpluses, a gross burden on taxpayers and consumers, and degradation of the rural landscape with encroachment by cultivation on fast disappearing wildlife habitats.' The debate has been led by a series of books, first *The theft of the countryside* by Marion

174

Shoard (1980), then two by Richard Body, *Agriculture: the triumph and the shame* (1982) and *Farming in the clouds* (1984), and *Agriculture, the countryside and land use* by John Bowers and Paul Cheshire (1983). The perception of farmers by the public, and the whole agricultural industry, has been transformed. As Lord Moran said in a debate in the House of Lords in May 1985 'Farmers are especially privileged people. They have very substantial grants and subsidies, guaranteed prices, their own tame Ministry. Indeed it was pointed out during the miners' strike that the farmers already have what Mr Scargill tried and failed to get; namely uneconomic farmers kept going by Government support!'

Lord Melchett, the Labour peer, has described MAFF as the pea brain of the dinosaur of agricultural policy, sending the industry to destruction. None the less, MAFF has moved under the pressure of criticism, although Hector Munro was perhaps exaggerating a little wildly when he told the Commons in February 1985 that 'following the Wildlife and Countryside Act 1981, the Ministry of Agriculture, Fisheries and Food had the greatest conversion since St Paul to nature conservation and the improvement of the habitat'.

This was certainly not the view of the House of Lords Select Committee on the European Community. Their report in July 1984 *Agriculture and the environment* was strongly critical of MAFF and its environmental policies (or lack of them). It is to this report that the subsequent (and surprisingly successful) attempt to amend the EEC Agricultural Structures Regulation can be attributed. MAFF claims to have increased its active concern for conservation. Section II of the Countryside Act 1968 gave them (along with every other government department) the duty to 'have regard to the desirability of conserving the natural beauty and amenity of the countryside'. While Section 41 of the Wildlife and Countryside Act requires the Agricultural Development and Advisory Service (ADAS) to extend its advice to farmers on 'the conservation and enhancement of the natural beauty and amenity of the countryside'. The government's White Paper responding to the House of Commons Select Committee Report on the Act stated blithely that 'Conservation has formed an element of the Ministry's advisory policy for many years'. It also said that 'There is broad agreement that farmers generally are showing an increasingly positive attitude towards conservation. Much of the credit for this is due to the painstaking effort of the ADAS in bringing home to farmers the conservation message'. While this may be one interpretation, the Select Committee itself said 'while there has undoubtedly been a welcome shift of emphasis in MAFF we are not convinced that MAFF has moved nearly far enough. We are disturbed that the policy makers are dragging their feet where they should be leading'.

MAFF's change of policy, or change of heart, over conservation is clearly very much in the eye of the beholder. In terms of substantive action, an environment co-ordination unit was established within MAFF in 1984, and in December 1984 the list of works for which capital grant would be available was changed, with the effect of promoting some developments beneficial to the environment rather than those damaging to it. Following the new EEC Structures Regulation the schedule of activities eligible for grant aid was revised again in July 1985. Before December 1984, grants had been available for hedge removal: now a 30% grant is available for hedge planting, tree planting or traditional walling, rising to 60% in LFAs, and there is no grant for land clearance. Given the scale of impacts of agricultural development on semi-natural habitats this can be seen as tokenism, but it is obviously a change in the right direction. Similarly, a 25% grant is now available for the alteration of farm buildings for tourism or craft purposes in LFAs, some indication of a move by MAFF to shoulder responsibility for the wider rural economy.

Despite these developments, MAFF is still far from convincing conservationists of its good intentions. In the debate of the Wildlife and Countryside (Amendment) Bill in the Commons in February 1985, John Gilbert MP said 'I am still very concerned about the general attitude displayed by the Ministry of Agriculture, Fisheries and Food ... I have been given a selection of adjectives or epithets which come from conservation groups. They describe their impression of the Ministry's attitude. There are descriptions such as, "wholly unsympathetic to environmental issues", "devious", "hostile", "indifferent", "bored", and "ignorant"'. In introducing the Bill, David Clark MP gave MAFF credit for its progress, but went on to argue that it needed 'a little push'. He said 'The whole point about bureaucrats and the official machinery is that their own inertia keeps them where they are'. In the event MAFF successfully shrugged off this helping hand. The clause in the Bill which gave it the duty to further nature conservation was excised at the Committee stage, although only by eight votes to seven. Both the then Under Secretary of State for the Environment, William Waldegrave, and the Parliamentary Secretary to MAFF, Peggy Fenner, were on the Committee, and spoke of the overlap between MAFF and the DOE which the clause would bring. Nicholas Bonser asked why the government should be frightened of the clause. Farmers needed to make an adequate return, but, he said 'anything we can do to encourage farmers to put that return back into the land in conservation form and not merely in forms which enhance the productivity of their land to grow crops or raise animals must be wholly desirable'. Arguments did not convince, and the clause was voted out. Despite extensive debate in the Lords in June 1985, the Bill went through in its amended (and reduced) form.

One problem for MAFF has been that it has moved more slowly than the CLA and the NFU, both of whom produced policy papers in the autumn of 1984 calling for a larger conservation element in agricultural policy. The Commons Select Committee commented 'It is ironic that an organisation like the NFU, whose first responsibility has always been to the success of the farmer, has to admit, whilst asserting that MAFF has been much maligned over the years, that "One has to recognise this is a major re-training policy for them and it will take a number of years to perhaps achieve what the ideal might be"'.

The NFU's policy statement *The way forward* was expanded in a more detailed paper in December 1984. The initiative was taken to make what it saw as a 'watershed', in postwar agricultural policy. The NFU saw the EEC as likely to follow a policy of financial restraint for agriculture. It acknowledged opposition to past policies over the countryside, pesticide pollution and animal welfare. Its new policies were based on the need to continue price support and to maintain incomes in agriculture and horticulture, and while they admitted that 'farmers and growers cannot be insulated from the effects of the attempt to achieve a better balance between supply and demand', it was stressed that 'political decisions must take account of the practical realities which face the farmer'. Surplus production should be controlled by a mix of quotas and price restraint, adjusted flexibly to suit different crops, and to protect British farmers against unfair EEC competition – especially from Spain and Portugal when they joined the Community. The NFU suggested that capital grant schemes should be amended to emphasise increased efficiency rather than increased production, to promote both the farm and non-farm income of small units, and to promote 'works designed to improve environmental protection, to enhance the appearance and amenity value of the countryside, and to safeguard animal welfare and wildlife'. Conservation was a major theme of *The way forward*. MAFF's attempts to amend the Structures Regulation were applauded, and the proper protection of SSSIs was supported, while planning controls were firmly rejected. Farmers wanted to conserve the countryside, but had businesses to run. The NFUs central message was clear, 'conservation costs money and will inevitably receive a low priority unless the industry is in a satisfactory financial position'.

The CLA proposals, which were in the form of a report of an advisory group and not official policy, were more radical. The group was appointed by the CLA's Agriculture and Land Use Sub-committee in March 1984 to look critically at agricultural policies and integration with environmental policies. They confirmed the need for the continuation of support for countryside enterprises to maintain farmers' incomes. Priority should be given to research on lower cost production systems, mixed farming systems which encourage diverse land use and environmental resource management, new crops and organic and 'natural' farming, and low-input low-output systems. Such systems were likely to be of interest to many farmers, but lack of information, and high fixed costs and mortgages made them unworkable. Quite simply 'the conservation benefit that could result would be hard to turn into cash for the farmer'.

The group had specific proposals for the capital grants system to direct agricultural funds away from raising food production towards wider countryside management, and away from the larger and wealthier farm business towards the small farmer. In detail, among other proposals, they suggested that the ceiling on grants should be lowered from £100 000 to £50 000 (to reduce the advantage to larger farmers), and grants should be confined to cost-reduction or environmental enhancement. Money saved should be diverted to support the maintenance of countryside features and provide advice, and to control agricultural pollution. Perhaps surprisingly, the group accepted planning control over farm roads and buildings, and – perhaps their most sweeping proposal – they suggested that MAFF's remit should be expanded to include responsibility for the NCC and the CC.

The CLA proposals are full of lively ideas, but of course are not formal policy. Both the CLA and the much more obviously self-interested NFU were chiefly pursuing the interests of their members but their endorsement of the idea that MAFF should give environmental and conservation matters higher priority in its policies and expenditure is important. To date MAFF has been very cautious indeed towards this point.

The shortcomings of MAFF's policies with regard to conservation were taken up in some detail by the House of Commons Select Committee on the Environment in its report on Part II of the 1981 Act, published on 16 January 1985. They recommended that conservation be given a greatly increased priority in the training and work of ADAS staff and that MAFF should increase its formal guidance on conservation. They recommended a working party to investigate MAFF's administrative structures to see how conservation could become a stronger element in agricultural policy, and called for financial structure to be fundamentally changed away from environmentally damaging operations towards conservation conscious methods. They called for a series of quite specific amendments to the 1981 Act, especially the blocking of the 'loopholes' and improved procedures for establishing marine nature reserves. They also called for a White Paper on the whole use of the 'rural estate'.

The Government's reply took four months to appear, by which time the Wildlife and Countryside (Amendment) Bill had been debated in the Commons, and been shorn of its clauses on Marine Nature Reserves and extra conservation duties for MAFF. It was a disappointment to conservationists, and an exercise in plastering blandly over cracks. It asserted 'Conservation is not now an optional extra with which land use and agricultural policies are decorated but is built into the structure of policy making as it should be'. The government was broadly happy to accept the recommendation about ADAS, largely because it argued that it dealt fully with conservation already. The working party on MAFF policy was not needed because conservation objections 'are now looked upon as being a major part of the ministry's overall responsibilities in pursuing a fair and balanced approach which takes due account of the needs of conservation, the agriculture industry and the consumer'. In calling for changes in agricultural support the Government suggested that the Committee had underestimated both the constraints caused by membership of the EEC, and the major progress already achieved. No radical changes were proposed. The call for a White Paper in the rural estate was again dismissed as superfluous: 'the Government will continue to respond appropriately to other current issues of public debate affecting agriculture and the rural environment.' Only on some of the specific issues of the Act's loopholes, and the need for further study of the Financial Guidelines, did the government response match the Committee's recommendation. Otherwise the report was courteously dismissed. There have apparently been 'major shifts in policy to the advantage of conservation' recently. In the government's view 'a healthier and balanced countryside policy must continue to rest upon the closer links between Departments which has led to these developments'.

These platitudes could well have been drafted by MAFF officials and sent out in the government's name. They show little regard for the intensity or direction of debate, which if anything has grown. In July 1985 the House of Lords Select Committee on the European Communities reported on the reform of the CAP. In 1983 the total EEC budget accounted for just under 1 per cent of the combined Gross Domestic Product of the community of 10 nations, and of the total budget of £14.5 billion fully two thirds (£9.7 billion) went on the CAP. The report said 'many, including farmers, have expressed concern that changes in farming practices and the development of modern agricultural techniques have been identified as a cause of the depletion and in some cases extinction of certain species of flora and fauna'. They also expressed a fear that advances in farming techniques 'could outstrip the Community's promotion of farming practices

designed to conserve the rural environment'. The Lords Committee concluded that on a number of grounds reform of the CAP was
imperative. In September 1985 Derek Barber, chairman of the CC,
renewed his call for public debate and clear government guidance
on the countryside, and the possible impacts (beneficial or
otherwise) of EEC policy changes. Despite government assurances
during 1985, concern about the future at the end of the year
remained acute in many quarters.

The impact of surplus

The government's recipe for the future of the countryside at the
end of 1985 seems to be more of the same, although a White
Paper on the rural estate is still a possibility, and DOE may
develop a package of proposals on environmental safeguards in
1986. There were also one or two interesting developments for
conservation towards the end of the summer of 1985. In September William Waldegrave was made Minister of Environment,
Conservation and Local Government, a move widely interpreted
as part of the government's attempt to court what is called 'the
green vote'. At the same period the Ecology Party changed its
name to the Green Party, and the Social Democratic Party
proposed a new Department of Environmental Protection. None
the less, it remains far from clear how this rush of enthusiasm for
green politics will affect conservation policy making in 1986, if
indeed it has any impact at all.

However, there will most certainly be policy developments in
the next year, of several kinds. The most significant is likely to
come from the EEC, and will involve measures to cut spending on
agriculture and to reduce overproduction and surpluses. The
Commission of the Economic Communities produced a green
paper in July 1985 presenting a number of basic options for the
future development of agricultural policy. Firm conclusions on
the future were due at the end of 1985, but the green paper made
clear the need for reorientation of the CAP and stressed the
political courage and sense of realism necessary to make useful
reforms. Among new perspectives, the Commission discussed the
role of agriculture in regional development, and as a protector of

181

the environment. Both would be novel directions for agricultural policy in Britain.

The measures for economic reform which may be proposed include production quotas, price control and possibly some kind of set-aside policy to reduce the area under certain crops. Any action will run into major difficulties in reconciling conflicting national interests, and these will only become more intractable with the accession of Spain, Portugal and Greece.

Milk is in many ways the most difficult commodity in surplus, partly because it is difficult to store, and partly because it is difficult to offload onto other markets. In March 1984 the EC set a quota for milk, requiring each country to cut production to 1981 levels plus 1%. This was intended to reduce the EEC surplus from 20% to 12%. It required a 6.5% cutback in Britain, 1.7% in France. Ireland negotiated a 4.5% increase in production on the grounds of hardship. As Britain was not quite self-sufficient in dairy products (unlike Denmark which exports two thirds of production) the quota system hit British farmers hard. Over 23 000 British dairy farmers applied to the special tribunal for remission. In the event, the dry summer of 1984 and payments (dubbed by the *Observer* 'golden milkshakes') of £650 per cow taken out of production, brought production in England and Wales down by some 200m litres, or 2% below the quota limit.

In the EEC as a whole milk powder production fell by 370 000 tonnes in 1984/85, and a further 200 000 tonnes fall is expected 1985/86. This represents a 25% cut back in production in just two years. None the less the milk quota has been unpopular, and the political power of farmers in countries like France is such that unpalatable policies may not be countenanced by governments.

The main issue in 1986, however, continues to be the overproduction of grain. 1984 saw a record harvest of 26.5 million tonnes of grain (5 million tonnes up on 1983, itself only just short of the previous record harvest in 1982). *The Times* put the cost of storing the 1984 surplus at about £30 million. Despite appalling harvest weather in 1985, by October there were 5.4 million tonnes of grain in store, and even low estimates in the press predicted a surplus of at least 2 million tonnes. Clearly the problems of grain surpluses persists. A 1.8% reduction in cereal price was agreed in July 1985, but with mitigation for Germany which, some commentators argued, more or less wiped out its effect. None the less, a policy of price control seems to be favoured over quotas. Another idea is to pay farmers to take land out of cereal production, this is known as a 'set aside' policy, and has been used (amidst much controversy) in the American prairies for some years. The NFU believe the idea cannot be transferred effectively to Europe, where so much depends on the maintenance of general market prices, and where the huge number of small farms and the diverse national administrative systems would create excessive bureaucratic costs.

Alan Buckwell, Professor of Agricultural Economics at Wye College, spoke to a conference run by the British Association of Nature Conservationists on set-aside policy in York in May 1985. He calculated that the surplus production of the EEC, chiefly in wheat, barley and milk, was such that at typical yields 5.3 million ha would need to be set aside in Europe. On current production, 18% of this would fall to Britain, a total of 0.94 million ha, (0.5 million ha of wheat, 0.4 million ha barley and 0.03 million ha of sugar). This is 5% of Britain's usable arable acreage. France would bear a larger burden (37% of the total), although Denmark would lose the largest percentage of its arable area (12%). Clearly he thought the proposal a political non-starter.

Whatever mechanism is adopted to attempt to control surplus production, it is inevitably going to have important effects on the countryside. Uncertainty over what will be done, and when, compounded by the hard political bargaining which is likely to occur, will make any policy formulation on conservation difficult. It is also likely to force MAFF back behind its Whitehall barricades, and may spell the end of the 'political ceasefire in the war between farmers and conservationists' heralded by John Young in *The Times* in May 1985. He predicts an uneasy truce 'likely to be interrupted by periodic sniping whenever some obdurate cereal farmer removes a 300-year-old hedge because it is keeping the sunlight off half an acre of winter wheat', but believes the atmosphere is 'notably less bellicose than a couple of years ago'.

The extent to which that ceasefire holds will be determined by the amount of money which flows to farmers in the name of conservation. From their point of view its source – in the NCC or MAFF – is a secondary concern, although it is likely that for it to be in any quantity at least part must come from the agriculture budget. MAFF has sufficient freedom under the Structures Regulation to move quite strongly into the support of conservation, particularly in the LFAs and through the provision for ESAs. If the NFU and CLA sense that there is money available for conservation while expenditure on increasing production is being restricted, they will push for it vigorously, and take their members with them. As John Young says in the same article 'cynics will say the only thing that has made many farmers supposedly more conservation conscious is that they are faced with falling prices, and probably with further restraints on production, not just of milk but of cereals as well'. Cynics or not, the logic is inescapable. For all their conservatism, farmers will welcome grants for conservation, if that is all that is on offer.

The effect of quotas or price restraint will not however be uniform across the country, nor would the impact of a set-aside policy. Unless they are specifically designed to favour the smaller and more marginal farmer, these measures will tend to divide Britain down the middle, roughly down the Severn–Tyne line. This will divide the richer, flatter and drier land – the old arable counties – in the South and East, from poorer, wetter land to the North and West. It is a pernicious division in many ways: farms in the South and East are on average larger and farmers more wealthy, this part of Britain is already most intensively farmed, and most affected by habitat loss. It is where most of the population (and most of the conservationists) live.

The effects of the three policies will be different in detail. Quotas will favour larger farmers over small, and more intensive units over less intensive. East of the line farms will tend to get larger, probably more mechanised. North and West of the line the fate of farmers will depend on the support for sheep and beef, but minor changes could push small farmers out of business. The likely effects of price control are clearer. In the East, larger farmers may respond by *increasing* production (to maintain income per ha), increasing the intensity and scale of production, while reducing costs. Agriculture will become still more industrialised, less in harmony with conservation. In the North and West again small farmers are likely to become uneconomic. A set-aside policy would obviously hit hardest in the counties producing surplus, i.e. the South and the East. However, beef and milk are also in surplus so land in the North and West might also need to be fallowed. Much of this land might go to forestry.

The implications of such changes for farmers are obviously considerable. The effect on nature conservation is also likely to be significant. As farm profitability falls, money for conservation is likely to be increasingly attractive. New capital grants for environmental enhancement, and management agreements which sustain appropriate agricultural production, will be a lifeline for many farm businesses. The North and West would become a land where agriculture exists primarily to maintain wildlife habitats and landscape beauty, and farm tourism and crafts dominate the economy. In the lowlands, however, the business of intensive production will go on, even if on a restricted area. The incompatibility between conservation and intensive agriculture will then develop a stronger regional dimension. There will be a tendency for increasing segregation between an area of intensive, profitable agriculture and an area of extensive low-input low-output conservation-orientated farming. It is very questionable whether this divided landscape is what is wanted in Britain, either for farming or conservation. We must return to it later, because it is exactly what policies of conservation site protection are themselves tending to produce.

Site protection

Whatever happens to agricultural policy, the Wildlife and Countryside Act will remain central to the protection of sssis. As agricultural receipts fall, demand for management agreements will rise. This will put greatly increased pressure on existing capabilities to renotify all sites and to process management agreements. In the lowlands, agricultural operations may intensify, and here the cost of agreements under the Guidelines will inevitably rise. The survival of the sssi system as it now stands depends on three things: the rapid completion of renotification, the removal of bottlenecks in the processing of agreements, and the provision of money to pay for agreements.

The NCC believes the task of renotification to be in hand. In the summer of 1984 Tony Patterson, author of *Conservation and the Conservatives*, suggested that the delay in renotification endangered the whole voluntary approach to site protection. His solution was to declare *all* sites renotified in the period before full documents could be served. This would probably not have been workable, and would not be judged superfluous: the NCC received an extra £2.25 million in July 1984 for site protection, and a further £7 million in November. They now predict completion by the end of 1986, meaning 80% renotification. Their own data suggest this is overly optimistic.

There are dangers in giving unrealistic guarantees, as well as failing to show progress after receiving extra money. Doubtless the NCC is aware of these: one can but repeat that until sites are notified under the Act *none* of its protection is extended to them. In fact they become *more vulnerable* to loss or damage, because some owners and occupiers will inevitably seize the chance to damage or destroy them before the jaws of bureaucracy close. The NCC told the House of Commons Environment Committee in November 1984 that it was too soon to judge the effectiveness of the 1981 Act. In large part that is because of their own difficulties in renotification, and the attendant delay. New AROs are being appointed, but will inevitably take time to become effective, and will stretch the NCC's internal management ability considerably. As they burrow into the mountain of case work, full renotification will creep slowly closer, but it will take time, probably until 1988, certainly till 1987. There are no shortcuts without radical restructuring of the legislation. The NCC is doing it right, but still not fast enough.

There is a similar problem over management agreements. They are complicated, take too long to negotiate, and the NCC is understaffed. This problem too is 'in hand', with attempts to recruit 10 more land agents in the autumn of 1985. There are problems in attracting the right people, and they will take time to learn the job. The bottleneck in concluding agreements will not readily be eased by this method. What is needed is some simple streamlining of the machiavellian complexity of the Financial

Guidelines. This is probably best done by some kind of standardised flat rate payment, backed up by a tribunal to investigate cases where landowners or occupiers feel hard done by. This would mean that when a farmer applies to carry out a potentially damaging operation, and is refused, there is a schedule of payments which includes the kind of change of operations he proposes, at a set rate per hectare. This should accelerate negotiations. It is not likely to reduce the overall cost of agreements, and runs the risk that farmers will feel that they deserve more than the standard payment because of their own circumstances, and will therefore refuse agreements. That is where a tribunal of some sort is needed, to keep such complaints within the field of negotiation. Unless this, or some other, way of streamlining the process of concluding agreements, is adopted, the central provision of the Act will not be effectively implemented. There are limits to the credibility of a system which allows a significant backlog of 'pending' agreements to build up. In the end, failure to process agreements will lead to the disaffection of owners and occupiers, and the damage or loss of sssis.

The final condition for some kind of 'success' with site protection under the Act as it now stands is that the government should continue to put the necessary money up for management agreements *and* for site acquisition. Politically they are fairly committed to doing so, although, as was discussed in Chapter 6, there are various ways of clouding the issue and wriggling out of their responsibilities. The most obvious is to call into question the NCC's judgement as to whether a particular sssi is worthy of protection in a particular way (compulsory purchase, protection by an S.29 order), another is to hide behind Whitehall expenditure restraint, a third for the secretary of state to accept arguments about economic benefits of development (somewhat hard in the case of arable farming: obviously easy in the case of whiskey distilling, as the case of Duich Moss clearly shows). When the government is disposed to duck difficult decisions, as they currently seem to be in Scotland, it is likely to be the potential of organisations like FOE to capture media attention which will keep money flowing to protect sssis, rather than the NCC's private anguish and entreaties behind the scenes. The loss of sssis was headline news through 1984 and 1985. Despite

187

the embarrassment and exasperation of NCC and landowners on occasions, it is vital that this remains so.

However, if anything breaks the government's commitment to the Act, and brings reform, it is likely to be the question of finance. The Act has brought a massively increased requirement for funds *in perpetuity*, for staff of the NCC to handle more case work, for agreements, and for site acquisition and maintenance. There will be very little slackening of any of these requirements even when renotification is complete. In 1984 Tony Patterson wrote 'It is sometimes said that the Act in its present form is unworkable. This is untrue. If the Government is prepared to pay out millions more pounds in compensation to the farmers for loss of subsidy, the Act is workable.' The sheer cost of site protection under the Act is such that there must be a query over the present government's continued willingness to pay. Certainly future governments of different political hue would probably take a very different line. This inevitably raises the question of more radical reform.

The most radical proposal is to make agricultural and forestry operations subject to planning control. It was chiefly this proposal from Marion Shoard in her book *The theft of the countryside* in 1980 which started the debate about the control of agricultural damage to conservation sites during the debate of the Wildlife and Countryside Bill. A leader in *The Times* in January 1985 commented 'The Act did not take the obvious route of planning control, which is the generally approved method of handling the impact of commercial development on the environment. Many think it should have, and do not believe that legislation short of that will ever be effective'. Agriculture is exempted from planning control under the General Development Order 1977. Many conservationists, notably FOE believe major agricultural and forestry operations should not be exempt. In their evidence to the House of Commons Select Committee, they proposed selective planning controls to cover new commercial forestry plantations, the felling of ancient or broadleaved woodlands, the ploughing of old meadows, moorland or heath, new wetland drainage schemes, and new agricultural roads and buildings.

These are quite sane proposals. In their favour is the fact that local people would have a hand in decisions about their own environment, and that costly management agreement would be unnecessary. FOE also believe that such planning controls, linked to reform of agricultural policy would be effective, where other approaches (including the present system) would not. It is commonly argued against planning controls that they would be grossly bureaucratic, and that planners would be ignorant of farming. Neither is a sound argument. Nothing would exceed the bureaucracy already demanded by the 1981 Act, and unlike the NCC, planning authorities have considerable experience in processing applications of this sort. There would be no difficulty in planners developing the necessary expertise quickly, especially as it is only fairly major changes in land use which would be controlled. By the same token, monitoring and enforcement would be fairly straightforward. Agriculture is no more complex than the industries and activities already controlled.

A more worrying argument is whether planning controls would in fact be effective, given the domination of local authorities in country areas by farmers. Opponents point to the very considerable proportion of SSSI damage and loss caused by activities which ought to be stoppable by planning. In some cases the problem is illegal action (e.g. tipping). This points to the need for thorough monitoring and effective enforcement of countryside controls. In many other cases, damage is caused by an agency or decision at central government level, such as the Coal Board, the gas or electricity boards, or the Department of Transport. Here the problem is not a failure of planning as much as a lack of concern for conservation – and to the duties laid down in Section 11 of the Countryside Act 1968 – on the part of government agencies. This is a serious problem, but should not be laid at the door of planning. The planning system does in fact work reasonably well in protecting the countryside in general. There is no reason to suppose that it would not work equally well if extended to agriculture and forestry.

The real benefit of planning controls of the sort FOE suggest would be felt in what is called 'the wider countryside', i.e. outside SSSIs and national parks. It would not guarantee the survival of every SSSI, however, so the provision for management agreements of some sort would be needed. Planning controls would also seem to be about the only possible defence against extensive afforestation, since as we have seen the financial guidelines do not provide an effective basis for agreements in such cases.

There are other alternatives to the present form of the 1981 Act which fall short of planning controls. One simple change in the provision of the Financial Guidelines would have a major effect both in simplifying management agreement procedures and avoiding the costly charade of annual index-linked payments. This would be to remove the option of annual payments. The Guidelines are based on the ideas of Lord Porchester on Exmoor in 1977. He proposed that farmers refused permission to plough moorland should be compensated once with a capital sum equivalent to the loss of capital value of the land owing to the restriction. This principle could be adopted for all management agreements under the 1981 Act. It would be equitable, easy to introduce, and far simpler than the present system to administer. There would be complications, for example over the position of tenants, but these would not be insuperable. There would also need to be more money available for separate annual agreements for *positive management* only, and also for purchase (compulsory or otherwise), to meet the circumstance of owners unable to accept the lump sum payment.

A third proposal would be even easier to implement. Payments under the Guidelines involve the assumption that agricultural grant would have been paid, and the NCC ends up paying for the equivalent of that grant in the name of conservation. This is widely agreed to be anomalous, indeed ridiculous, although there is a danger that if the viability of a farming regime is wholly dependent on grant aid, and the management agreement ignores that, the farmer is unlikely to accept it. Even if he wished to, he might be financially unable to do so. None the less, it would be simple to amend the Guidelines to exempt grant payments from the calculation. This might cut up to 25% off the bill for management agreements. While this proposal (like the other two) is hardly likely to be wholly popular with farmers, it is arguably only reasonable since if MAFF is serious about its duty to have regard to nature conservation, it should not give grants in SSSIs anyway.

A different approach to SSSI protection is the extension of

ownership by conservation bodies. It is possible to calculate that if management agreements are going to cost £20 million a year, then after 50 years £1000 million will have been spent protecting the sssi system. These figures are based on the assumption that one third of the area of the sssi system is either of negligible value or is already held by conservation agencies, and that only half of the rest would require management agreements. Thus about £1000 million (and this is one of the lower guesstimates) would be spent over 50 years to protect about 0.7 million ha of sssi land. This is the equivalent of an average of £1400 per ha. Given that much of the land in sssis is of poor quality, this would be enough to buy it.

So if the government is actually serious about protecting sssis (and not simply appearing to protect them, which is probably nearer the truth) for more than 50 years, it might be cheaper to buy them. NCC policy is still to acquire all the sites listed in the 1977 Nature Conservation Review (plus a few others which have been found since then), and its first Corporate Plan sets targets for the next 10 years. None the less, they appear to shrink from the idea of acquisitions on a larger scale. Partly, this is through fear of the public relations impact of appearing to want to 'sterilise' (a commonly wielded phrase) anything like 10% of Britain. Partly it is because they fear the cost of management of small parcels of land outside a larger farm operation. Many sssis are small, and many are of value because of traditional agricultural practices which would need to be continued. The NCC is tied to Civil Service salaries and accounting procedures, and does not have the freedom to operate in an entrepreneurial spirit. Average costs of management are £15–20 per ha on NCC reserves, 50–80% of their guess of the eventual *average* cost of agreements. The official NCC view seems to be that it simply is not worth the cost and the bother of acquiring large numbers of sssis as reserves. They also forsee insuperable difficulties in asking for a billion pounds for conservation in one lump: in terms of practical Whitehall politics, it just can't be done, except perhaps by the Ministry of Defence.

The trouble with this argument is that, if carried to its logical conclusion, it undermines the NCC's only real sanction where a site is threatened by an obdurate landlord: compulsory purchase. A number of sites have been acquired since 1980 simply because they were threatened, and NNR status was the only way to protect them. Of course, these sites were all important, but their priority for acquisition was the result primarily of threat. They include Blar Nam Faoileag in Caithness (threatened by afforestation now held under NRA), Elmley Farm in Kent (threatened by drainage, NRA being negotiated), and the Ribble estuary (threatened by reclamation for agriculture in 1979, purchased). The Act will inevitably increase the number of sites which need to be protected in this way. The NCC has to be prepared to act vigorously to acquire sites not at the top of its shopping list, and the government will have to pay the price unless it wishes to risk being accused of refusing the protection it has promised.

It would not demand a major shift in policy to extend this site acquisition process. One approach would be to set a ceiling on management agreements, and for the NCC to seek to buy sites which rose above this. Another would be for the NCC to increase its support of SSSI purchase by voluntary conservation bodies. Currently the NCC can give 25% of the purchase price of an SSSI to voluntary bodies (33% of a Nature Conservation Review site) but only if the purchase price is not above the District Valuer's figure for the land's worth. This is a problem, for very often the District Valuer's estimate is less than an owner is willing to sell for. In practice, if the RSPB or a County Naturalists' Trust wants to buy the site, they have to do it without help. It would be relatively easy for the DOE to allow the NCC to pay larger grants (50% or 75%), and to pay them even if the purchase price is over the District Valuer's valuation (perhaps at a set percentage of the District Valuer's price). In the long run this might push up land prices, but on the relatively small scale likely, this would probably have little effect. In this way, more sites would be brought into explicit conservation management, the costs of maintenance falling on the voluntary contributions of members of the various associations.

One other development which would have a fairly dramatic effect on the success of nature conservation would be the reorientation of agricultural grants. This was proposed by Clive Potter, now at Wye College in Kent, in 1983 in a report published by the World Wildlife Fund called *Investing in rural harmony*. He proposed an 'Alternative Package of Agricultural Subsidies'

(APAS for short), which would adjust the way agricultural grant was given, but without altering the overall size of the grants budget. Given the moves within the agricultural industry towards conservation during 1984, it is perhaps surprising that his ideas have received relatively little attention, despite a Royal Society of Arts Seminar in April 1984 which assembled national authorities to discuss them. One reason for this might be what Tim O'Riordan, Professor of Environmental Studies at the University of East Anglia, calls the element of 'environmental Robin Hoodism' in Clive Potter's proposals, 'a transfer of resources from the agriculturally wealthy to agriculturally (and in conservation terms) the more deserving'.

Clive Potter's approach was to focus on target groups within agriculture. Those with land of high conservation value would be eligible for 'special area' grants and subsidies designed to achieve conservation objectives *and* maintain farm incomes. In the LFAS headage payments would be adjusted to reward poorer farmers and to promote landscape conservation. In the wider countryside, advice and grants would be aimed at farm investment (not single projects), and should try to bring conservation 'out of the field corner' and into the mainstream of decision making and policy.

These proposals are distinct from the debate about reducing the overall cost of agricultural support (which is largely determined by subsidies). To an extent the idea of ESAs works in a similar way. It has the great advantage that (unlike APAS) it is actually already part of operational policy. Its impact remains to be seen. Obviously, the agricultural industry has moved some small way towards these kind of ideas in a number of areas since 1983, especially with the NFU and CLA policy statements of 1984 and the new Agricultural Structures Regulations, while small farmers have become quite fashionable as the NFU wakes up to the fact that their membership is falling. It is clear that further reform of farm grants could bring substantial benefits of nature conservation as well as landscape conservation, although many organisations may well need a considerably greater fund of economic skill before they can suggest workable proposals. Obviously the reform of the agricultural grants structures should be part of any package of reform.

There are, then, a series of possible ways in which the Act and

193

the guidelines could be amended to make site protection more effective. Some are more controversial than others. Some combination is likely to be needed. The following package of measures is suggested:

(a) Confine all obligatory payments for management agreements to a lump-sum payment for loss of the capital value of the land. Review of the Guidelines annually by Parliament.
(b) Expand the use of voluntary management agreements to provide specific desirable management of SSSIs.
(c) Extend grant support and incentives for SSSI acquisition by voluntary bodies.
(d) Introduce selective planning controls on agricultural and forestry land use to cover the felling of ancient woodlands, the ploughing of moor, heath, or herb-rich meadows, the planting of blocks of conifers, and agricultural and forestry roads and buildings.
(e) Reform agricultural grant and support structures to promote conservation management directly and to help less wealthy farmers.
(f) Develop the concept of ESAs and extend their coverage to include a significant proportion of SSSIs.

Idealistic packages like this are rarely satisfactory, and details can be debated indefinitely. The main point, however, is simple. The 1981 Act alone will not prevent the loss of SSSIs, but will only slow it, and will do that expensively. Something stronger is needed, and there is no administrative magic wand which can be waved to do what is necessary. Both the NCC and the CC are wrong, it *is* early enough to judge the 1981 Act. It is inadequate, and it needs reform. However this will not be simple. It will almost certainly require a package of measures carefully adjusted to fit the changing policies in agriculture and forestry.

Integration or exclusion?

The Wildlife and Countryside Act in its present form is likely to fall short of the aim of protecting the SSSI system. Even if it can be

194

amended, or augmented, to achieve this aim, it is still very questionable whether this is enough. The Act has altered the status of SSSIS from a rather nebulous designation scattered fairly generally across the countryside in the hope that other land users would respect them, to a tightly defined series of sites whose characteristics, boundaries and management needs are known and maintained. The Act acknowledged the fact that intensive agriculture and forestry are not compatible with conservation, and effectively extended the area in which NCC approved management was carried out from the NNR series (less than 0.2 million ha) to the SSSI system (about 2 million ha). SSSIS will, when renotification is complete, cover about 10% of Britain. This is not enough.

There are many sites quite rich in wildlife which are not judged worthy of SSSI status. This might simply be because the rather ridiculous idea of representativeness persists in SSSI selection, and of two similar sites only one may be chosen. Alternatively it may be that an area fails to qualify as an SSSI simply because it is rather ordinary, not exceptional or special. This does not mean it is not valuable. One example of this kind of problem is demonstrated in the NCC's Ancient Woodlands Inventory. This has details of all ancient woodlands, woods which have been in existence since AD 1600. They tend to have a high species diversity, and species uncommon elsewhere, and are of enormous interest to conservationists. However, many have been damaged by recent forestry practices, especially the planting of conifers, and many are not SSSIS. The inventory acts rather like a parallel SSSI schedule of special, but not nationally special, woodland sites. How are those which are not SSSIS to be protected?

One solution is to extend the protection given to SSSIS – the need for reciprocal notification, the provision for a Section 29 Order, etc. – to sites such as those. This may very well be worth it, but it fails to solve the problem. What of other areas not on any particular list? What of the ordinary countryside? The fact is that the 1981 Act is exclusive in its working. It focuses attention on the SSSI system, it tries (for all its faults) to promote the conservation of that system, but it does very little for the wider countryside. Kenneth Carlisle MP made the point clearly to the Commons in February 1985: 'Isolated SSSIS dotted around the country like oases in the desert are inadequate. The intervening farmland must also provide habitat'.

The inadequacy of any conservation policy which only protects sssis is both biological and practical. If sssis are protected and yet the wildlife interest of the land surrounding them continues to decline, they will become increasingly isolated islands in an increasingly inhospitable sea of incompatible land use. There is now a large literature on island biogeography which discusses the low rate of immigration of species to small isolated islands. The scientific debate on this has become very convoluted, partly because there has been too much theorising and far too little empirical study, but the basic principles are fairly widely accepted. The smaller and more remote an island, the less likely it is that any species which goes extinct will reinvade or that new species will appear of their own accord. The small population will be vulnerable to natural catastrophe (for example a heath fire could wipe out an isolated population of smooth snakes), and may suffer from problems of a small gene pool. The relevance of these ideas to habitat islands and reserves has been the subject of intense and sometimes acrimonious debate in the literature. The implications are, however, that there may be many problems with trying to preserve the British fauna and flora within the sssi system, even if it extends to 10% of the country.

There are also practical problems for conservation in the 'divided landscape'. It is quite clear that the success of conservation depends on public support. To date it is the conservation of landscape which has won the reputation of being 'for the people'. The conservation of nature in sssis on private land will not have much appeal. People will want to know that these 'gems' are not being destroyed, but they will also want to see conservation in action for themselves. This may demand action on access to sssis (a thorny problem for the NCC), but it will certainly also mean that wildlife has to be found a place in the wider countryside.

This will be far from easy to achieve. One of the most persistent myths about conservation is that it is compatible with intensive agriculture and intensive forestry. It is not. The word 'compromise' in this context sadly means strategic withdrawal for conservation. As William Wilkinson, chairman of the NCC, commented in *Natural selection* in 1985 'nature conservation has recently, despite a spirited rearguard action, been one long retreat'. The 1981 Act does little to achieve any place for conservation outside the sssi system. As the CPRE said in their evidence to the House of Commons Environment Committee in 1984 'Changes to the Wildlife and Countryside Act alone will not secure the degree of integration that is necessary to reduce conflicts in the countryside'.

The answer has to be integration: a policy of exclusion alone will create a 'nature conservation landscape' which is inadequate in both ecological and human terms. And yet somehow this 'integration' has to be achieved without the familiar defeat for conservation. This is quite clearly what happened in the case of the Berwyn Mountains in mid-Wales. This enormous upland area (some 155 000 ha) has important breeding bird populations, and in 1977 the RSPB suggested that 60 000 ha be declared an sssi. Instead the NCC in Wales appointed a consultant to draw up a land use plan for the area to take into account the powerful and vociferous farming and forestry interests. In what might either be regarded as a classic piece of land use planning or a predictable response to the relative power of the different interests, the NCC eventually decided to notify an sssi in 1982 of less than 14 000 ha. An area of some 8000 ha apparently of sssi quality was excluded, and all sorts of informal agreements made with farmers there. This is an old story. In 1982 Chris Rose and Charles Secrett called the notification 'a serious scientific miscalculation by the NCC'. They might have called it a lack of nerve. Whatever the truth of the situation, it is clear in this instance that co-operation and integration are euphemisms for retreat and defeat.

Another example of what is *not* needed in the way of integration is the set of so-called 'Integrated Development Programmes' in the Outer Isles, Shetland and Orkney. That in the Outer Isles was first. It is overall an excellent programme, 80% funded by the EEC and pumping some much needed money into the depressed economy of the Hebrides. Its 'Integration' however did not extend to environmental conservation. The NCC was involved in planning from an early stage, but was effectively marginalised into a position where it was not able to influence the way the £20 million was spent. It can only object to developments on sssis (under the Act). If it objects elsewhere, the Department of Agriculture either sits on the objection, ignores the NCC or turns down the grant application, none of which is helpful to the crofters who will not then necessarily be offered a management agreement. In fact, of the £20 million, only £3.6 million was earmarked for land improvement, and of this £3 million was taken up with alacrity for fencing. This has had little environmental impact, so the whole programme has fortuitously harmed the wildlife of the Outer Isles very little. Had circumstances been different, the lack of any environmental appraisal or maintenance money in the original programme (DOE belatedly gave £30 000 for an Environmental Impact Assessment) could have been disastrous. Worst of all, fears about possible opposition from the NCC to developments has produced a deep and apparently abiding rift between the NCC and crofters. A more harmful project for conservation would be hard to imagine.

Relations between NCC and local people have also been seriously impaired in Shetland and Orkney. Here the investment is predominantly local money from oil revenues, but again part of it is going to land improvement. Rough grazing is being enclosed and reseeded, and managed intensively. Agriculturally such developments make little sense. They favour the larger farms, and if continued will do in the islands what MAFF policy has done in England, and push farmers off the land. Ironically, the investment may do more damage to the local lifestyle than the NCC's objections to development are said to do. The problem is acute: 70% of the island of Fetlar for example (where the Snowy Owl bred) is sssi, and since the roll-on roll-off ferry was introduced 10 years ago there have been no part-time jobs on the island (with the GPO, or the old boat service to the steamer). The only alternative for the crofters is to expand their farm. They see the NCC's opposition to the development of land within sssis as a direct attack on their survival. The island Councils, many of whose policies lie at the root of the problem, speak of the 'spreading green slime' of conservation. It has become a bitterly polarised situation: no model of integration.

These examples do, however, point the way towards a solution. The CPRE said in 1984 'conservation objectives in the

National Parks and the wider countryside need to be expressed through, rather than achieved in opposition to, policies governing agriculture and forestry.' What is needed are integrated policies, not attempts to meld incompatible policies. That way lies conflict and – to be realistic – defeat for conservation. This is, of course, the message of the world conservation strategy (WCS), although it can seem on some lips a cynical and trivial, or blindly idealistic one. In 1982, the World Wildlife Fund financed a British response to the WCS, and a series of seven reports were researched and discussed. They varied in quality and depth of perception, but some were very good. The whole exercise was largely ignored by the media, and to date little interest has been shown by government. The paper on rural resources, 'Putting trust in the countryside', was written by Tim O'Riordan of the University of East Anglia. It came up with an overflowing basket of interlocking proposals to make rural land use sustainable in terms of the capacity of ecosystems to continue to produce both physical goods and the less commercial products of wildlife and landscape. This approach needs far more sustained thought from conservationists, if the short-term adversarial tactics of the past 10 years are ever to be replaced by longer-term planning.

There are just one or two glimmers of hope on the horizon, and some examples of how new integrated policies might work. The CC and Peak District National Park have launched a scheme in the parishes of Longnor and Monyash with a holistic package of management agreements to conserve the area. One scheme allows payment of a per hectare sum on the basis of the species diversity of hay meadows, for example. This sounds rather fanciful but it seems to work. The idea needs to be tried elsewhere. Similarly, the experiment funded by the CC and MAFF on the Halvergate Marshes in Norfolk with payments to farms to stay in traditional low-intensity beef production, needs to be carefully evaluated and followed up. Both of these initiatives fall into the purlieu of the CC, but there is no reason why the approach is unsuited to nature conservation and the NCC. The new 'ESA', introduced in the Structures Directive March 1985 may provide an avenue for developments of this sort, and for co-operation across the 'great divide' which – as Ann and Malcolm MacEwen have described –

lies damagingly deep and wide between 'amenity' and nature conservation.

Government policy, and the awareness and activities of conservation bodies, have changed greatly since the passage of the Wildlife and Countryside Act 1981, and the whole field has changed out of all recognition since the debates about the countryside in the 1940s. However, any attempt simply to graft new measures for conservation onto the old is, in the long run, going to be unsatisfactory. Agriculture and forestry policy have been evolving for the last 60 years and more, and long before that they have been moulding the social and environmental conditions of the countryside. Piecemeal interventions will achieve little: what is needed is a holistic view and courageous policy-making across a diverse range of related fields.

The problems of the countryside are complex and closely interrelated. It is no longer good enough to try to distinguish between the social and environmental aspects of rural policy, and to deal with them in watertight boxes. The British government will have to follow the direction in which the EEC seems to be looking, and to grasp the nettle of tackling rural economy, welfare and environment in an integrated way. This will mean at the very least some rationalisation of the role of MAFF to integrate it with the DOE's responsibilities for environmental protection and enhancement.

To stop habitat loss, and create the kind of countryside we want in Britain, we must look to far more dynamism and initiative from the NCC, but also beyond that to new and supporting government policies for the countryside. Unless the government is prepared to develop effective rural policies, the future for nature conservation and habitat protection will be bleak. New approaches to old divisions and conflicts will also be required. Theo Burell, who retired in 1985 after 16 years as chief officer of the Peak District National Park, wrote in *Countryside Commission News* in June 1985, 'to succeed, public authorities must completely change their style of working. Departmental success should be measured by the extent to which joint work with other departments has been achieved. It should not be judged on frontiers defended, or limited horizons'.

It remains to be seen whether change of this sort is possible.

One thing is quite certain, that the prime need is for continued public pressure to back conservation and its statutory and voluntary agencies. The message of the past is clear: if the spirit is willing much can be achieved, even if for the moment the flesh and the legislation remain grievously weak.

Further reading

Body, R. 1982. *Agriculture: the triumph and the shame*. London: Temple Smith.

Body, R. 1984. *Farming in the clouds*. London: Temple Smith.

Bowers, J. and P. Cheshire 1983. *Agriculture and the countryside and land use*. London: Methuen.

O'Riordan, T. 1983. Putting trust in the countryside. In *The conservation and development programme for the UK: a response to the world conservation strategy*, (eds.) UK Conservation and development programme organising committee, 171–260. London: Kogan Page.

Patterson, T. 1984. *Conservation and the Conservatives*. A Bow Paper.

Potter, C. 1983. *Investing in rural harmony: an alternative package of agricultural subsidies and incentives for England and Wales*. Godalming, Surrey: World Wildlife Fund.

Shoard, M. 1980. *Theft of the Countryside*. London: Temple Smith.

Appendix: Potentially damaging operations (February 1983)

1   Cultivation (including ploughing, rotovating, harrowing and re-seeding).

2   Grazing [where already damaging] or the introduction of grazing [where applicable]. Changes in the grazing regime (including type of stock or intensity or seasonal pattern of grazing and cessation of grazing).

3   Stock feeding [where already damaging] or the introduction of stock feeding [where applicable]. Changes in stock feeding practice.

4   Mowing or other methods of cutting vegetation [where already damaging], or the introduction of mowing, etc. [where applicable]. Changes in the mowing or cutting regime (including hay making to silage and cessation).

5   Application of manure, fertilisers and lime.

6   Application of pesticides, including herbicides (weedkillers).

7   Dumping, spreading or discharge of any materials.

8   Burning and changes in the pattern or frequency of burning [where applicable].

9   The release into the site of any wild, feral or domestic animal, including pest control ('animal' includes any mammal, reptile, amphibian, bird, fish or invertebrate).

11 The destruction, displacement, removal or cutting of any plant or plant remains, including (e.g. tree, shrub, herb, hedge, dead or decaying wood, moss, lichen, fungus, leaf-mould, turf, etc.).

12   Tree and/or woodland management* [where already damaging], or the introduction of tree and/or woodland management* [where applicable]. Changes in tree and/or woodland management (*including afforestation, planting, clear and selective felling, thinning, coppicing, modification of the stand or underwood, changes in species composition, cessation of management).

13a   Drainage (including moor-gripping and the use of mole, tile, tunnel or other artificial drains).

13b   Modification of the structure of water courses (e.g. rivers, streams, springs, ditches, dykes, drains), including their banks and beds, as by re-alignment, regrading and dredging.

13c   Management of aquatic and bank vegetation for drainage purposes [see also 11].

14   The changing of water levels and tables and water utilisation (including irrigation, storage and abstraction from existing water bodies and through boreholes).

15   Infilling of ditches, dykes, drains, ponds, pools, marshes or pits.

16a   Freshwater fishery production and/or management, including sport fishing and angling [where already damaging], or the introduction of freshwater fishery production and/or management. Changes in freshwater fishery production and/or management, including sport fishing and angling.

16b   Coastal fishing or fisheries management and seafood or marine life collection, including the use of traps or fish cages [where already damaging], or the introduction of coastal fishing [where applicable]. Changes in coastal fishing practice or fisheries management and seafood or marine life collection.

17   Reclamation of land from sea, estuary or marsh.

18   Bait digging in intertidal areas [England and Wales only].

19   Erection of sea defences or coast protection works, including cliff or landslip drainage or stabilisation measures.

20   Extraction of minerals, including peat, shingle, sand and gravel, topsoil, subsoil, chalk, lime, limestone pavement, shells and spoil.

21   Construction, removal or destruction of roads, tracks, walls, fences, hardstands, banks, ditches or other earthworks, or the laying, maintenance or removal of pipelines and cables, above or below ground.

22   Storage of materials.

23   Erection of permanent or temporary structures, or the undertaking of engineering works, including drilling.

24   Modification of natural or man-made features (including cave entrances), clearance of boulders, large stones, loose rock or scree and battering, buttressing or grading rock-faces and cuttings, infilling of pits and quarries.

25   Removal of geological specimens, including rock samples, minerals and fossils.

26   Use of vehicles or craft likely to damage or disturb features of interest.

27   Recreational or other activities likely to damage features of interest.

28   Game and waterfowl management and hunting practices [where already damaging], or introduction of game or waterfowl management [where applicable]. Changes in game and waterfowl management and hunting practice.

Index